# Banking Unchained

## How Cryptocurrencies Can Transform Your Financial Life

**Lev Mikulitski & Matías Monteagudo**

# Banking Unchained

LEV MIKULITSKI

MATIAS MONTEAGUDO

COVER DESIGN by LEV MIKULITSKI

WWW.MIKULITSKI.COM

INFO@MIKULITSKI.COM

# DEDICATION

This book is dedicated to those who find themselves on a relentless quest for innovative tools that have the power to enrich and elevate their lives. To the dreamers who dare to envision a future unbounded by the limitations of the present; to the bold who courageously chase after novel opportunities, undeterred by the risks that lie in the path of innovation; and to the indefatigable spirits who, time and time again, rise to meet the challenges that accompany the pursuit of groundbreaking frontiers.

To those who harbor an insatiable curiosity, a hunger for knowledge that propels them forward in a world ever-evolving, ever-expanding in its complexities and wonders. To the pioneers, venturing into the unknown with a heart full of hope and a mind open to the limitless possibilities that the world of cryptocurrencies unfolds.

# CONTENTS

## LEGAL DISCLAIMER

The information contained in "Banking Unchained: How Cryptocurrencies Can Transform Your Financial Life" (hereinafter referred to as "the Book") is for educational and informational purposes only. It is derived from the authors' personal experiences and their understanding of the cryptocurrency landscape. While the authors have taken due diligence in ensuring the accuracy and completeness of the information presented, they make no representations or warranties of any kind, express or implied, about the completeness, accuracy, reliability, suitability, or availability with respect to the Book or the information, products, services, or related graphics contained in the Book for any purpose. Any reliance you place on such information is therefore strictly at your own risk.

The Book does not offer investment advice, financial guidance, or advocate the purchase, retention, or sale of any asset, security, or commodity. It does not promise or guarantee any specific outcome or profit, and you should be aware that you can lose money. The cryptocurrency market is highly volatile and investing in it carries risk. It is important to note that past performance is not indicative of future results.

The authors are not financial advisors, brokers, or dealers. They are not members of any financial or commodities regulatory body and do not hold any formal qualifications to give financial advice. Before making any investment decisions, you are advised to consult with a qualified and registered financial advisor and undertake your own due diligence and independent research.

The authors and publishers of the Book disclaim and exclude all liability to the fullest extent permitted by law for any losses, damages, costs, or expenses, whether direct or indirect, incurred or suffered by any person arising out of or in connection with the use of or reliance on any of the contents of this Book.

The Book may contain references to third-party websites, and the authors are not responsible for the content of those websites. The inclusion of any links does not necessarily imply a recommendation or endorse the views expressed within them.

By purchasing or using the Book, you agree that the authors and publishers will not be held liable for any actions you take based on the information contained within it. You acknowledge that you are using the information available in this Book at your own risk and that you are responsible for any decisions you make based on the information provided.

# INTRODUCTION

In the ever-evolving landscape of the 21st century, the world is witnessing a paradigm shift in the realm of finance. The advent of cryptocurrencies, a form of digital or virtual currency that uses cryptography for security, has sparked a revolution that is reshaping the global financial system. This revolution, while filled with immense potential, is also fraught with uncertainty and fear. It is this dichotomy that forms the crux of our exploration in this book, "Banking Unchained: How Cryptocurrencies Can Transform Your Financial Life".

As we stand on the brink of a new era, our world appears starkly divided. On one hand, some perceive cryptoassets (a more accurate term than cryptocurrencies) as a realm of volatility and risk, seemingly reserved for the tech-savvy and out of reach for the average person. While this viewpoint isn't baseless, it often stems from a lack of understanding and an aversion to change. Conversely, others champion cryptoassets as a revolutionary force poised to democratize finance, empower individuals, and drive business growth. While this perspective is hopeful, it also recognizes the hurdles ahead and the imperative for education, regulation, and robust infrastructure.

This book is a bridge between these two perspectives. It is a guide for individuals and small businesses who are intrigued by the promise of crypto assets but are unsure of how to navigate this new terrain. It is for those who are seeking financial freedom and a higher quality of life but are wary of the risks involved. It is for those who understand that the world is changing and want to be a part of that change, rather than being left behind.

We begin our journey by exploring the basics of cryptoassets, demystifying the technology, and laying a foundation for understanding how they can be integrated into our daily financial lives. We delve into the issues of security and privacy, providing practical advice on how to protect your assets in the digital world. We discuss investment strategies, highlighting the risks and rewards that come with venturing into the crypto market. We examine the regulatory landscape, offering insights into the complexities of global crypto laws and how to ensure compliance. We also explore the role of cryptoassets in promoting financial inclusion, particularly in regions where traditional banking systems are less accessible.

Navigating the dynamic landscape of cryptoassets, one quickly realizes it's not a remote or elusive domain. It's a burgeoning frontier, molded by audacious individuals and enterprises who dare to envision, innovate, and challenge conventional financial paradigms. Every newcomer, in their exploration and participation, plays a role in sculpting this nascent industry, teeming with untapped potential and uncharted possibilities. This digital ecosystem offers an unparalleled avenue toward financial freedom and prosperity, unhindered by the limitations of traditional finance.

In this transformative exploration of the crypto world, I am thrilled to be your guide. However, unlike my previous books where I was the sole voice, sharing insights and knowledge drawn from my own hands-on experiences, this time I've decided to take a different approach. Recognizing the vast and complex nature of the crypto landscape, I felt it was crucial to bring in an expert who has not only studied this field but has also been deeply involved in its practical applications.

I've invited my close friend and collaborator, Matías Monteagudo, to accompany us on this pivotal journey. While we share a partnership in Mellifex LLP—a distinctive technology tailored for executing unique crypto transactions, Matías's connection to the world of blockchain and cryptocurrencies spans over a decade.

His engagement goes beyond mere theory; it is deeply rooted in tangible, on-the-ground work. His expertise encompasses everything from a basic understanding of the technology to its innovative applications in numerous ventures. The insights Matías has amassed from his extensive hands-on experience in the crypto world are invaluable. Recently, he has lent his technical expertise to institutions such as the European Supervisory Authorities (EBA, EIOPA, and ESMA), representing the industry. More on that later.

Together, we will navigate the intricate labyrinth of the crypto world. Our dialogue, a blend of probing questions coupled with enlightening and deep answers, will form the backbone of this book. This format offers a unique and engaging way to delve into the world of cryptoassets from a different perspective, providing a comprehensive yet captivating look at the topic at hand. In our worldview, it's not just about imparting knowledge; it's about sparking curiosity, encouraging understanding, and inspiring you to explore the potential that cryptocurrencies hold for your financial future.

Some readers may discern the distinct writing styles present in this book — a reflection of our individual backgrounds. My articulation leans heavily towards American English, while Matías favours a British-tinged approach. We chose to retain our individual styles, allowing for a rich tapestry of perspectives that honour both the interviewer and the interviewee in their unique voices.

This book is structured as a series of interviews, each focusing on a key aspect of the crypto world. For the individual seeking to understand and potentially enter this realm, we will delve into topics such as understanding the basics of crypto assets, ensuring security and privacy, strategizing for investment and profit, navigating regulation and compliance, promoting financial inclusion, and understanding the environmental impact of cryptoassets. Each of these topics will provide you with the knowledge and tools you need to confidently step into the world of cryptoassets.

For the small business owner or entrepreneur, we will explore how cryptoassets can be adopted and integrated into your business model. We will discuss how crypto can enhance customer engagement, facilitate global commerce, manage risk, impact taxation and accounting, drive innovation and growth, and align with sustainability and ethical goals. These discussions will provide practical, actionable insights that can help transform your business and position it for success in the digital age.

As we explore these topics, we will not sidestep the challenges and complexities that come with the adoption of cryptoassets. Instead, we will tackle them directly, offering clear, honest, balanced and well-informed perspectives. Our aim is not to persuade you that cryptoassets are the cure-all for financial difficulties, but to equip you with the knowledge and understanding necessary to make informed decisions that align with your personal and business objectives. Moreover, we aim to provide insights that truly resonate with people like you, those who are striving for financial freedom and, ultimately, a better life.

Recognizing that this book will find its way to individuals who are either venturing into the crypto space for the first time or simply harboring a curiosity about the topic, we have chosen to incorporate a glossary at the end. This glossary elucidates selected technical terms, facilitating a smoother navigation through the professional jargon peppered throughout the book, and enhancing the reader's engagement and understanding.

To address the burning questions and concerns of those eager to delve into the world of crypto, yet feeling the timing isn't right, we've sought to deeply understand the main challenges and areas of uncertainty facing individuals like you, looking to navigate the crypto landscape. So, what drives individuals and businesses to the crypto domain? While motivations vary, many are drawn to the digital and crypto worlds due to frustrations with the conventional financial system. Here are some pivotal insights, based on recent studies and reports:

1. **Decentralization and Financial Freedom**: crypto assets are seen as a democratizing force that can wrest control of money creation and management from central banks and Wall Street. This is particularly appealing to people who feel marginalized or underserved by traditional financial institutions. Cryptoassets can be transferred relatively quickly and anonymously, even across borders, without the need for a bank that could block the transaction or charge a fee.

2. **Investment and Speculation**: Many people are drawn to cryptoassets because they see them as a potentially lucrative investment. Despite the high levels of volatility and risk, the possibility of significant returns can be a strong motivator. Some people buy cryptoassets because of a speculative belief that these tokens are going to go up in the future, as a new future is being built on the blockchain.

3. **Financial Inclusion**: cryptoassets, particularly stablecoins, have the potential to bring millions of people who lack traditional bank accounts into the financial system. They can be used by anyone with a smartphone, making them accessible to a wide range of people.

4. **Distrust in Traditional Financial Systems**: Some people are turning to cryptoassets because they lack confidence in the safety and reliability of traditional financial systems. A Pew Research Center survey found that among Americans who have heard about crypto assets, 75% say they are not confident that

current ways to invest in, trade, or use cryptocurrencies are reliable and safe.

5. **Protection Against Inflation**: Some investors see Bitcoin as a hedge against inflation because the supply is permanently fixed, unlike fiat currencies, which central banks can expand indefinitely.

However, it's crucial to note that while cryptoassets offer potential benefits, they also come with significant risks. These include market volatility, lack of regulatory clarity, potential for fraud, and cybersecurity threats. As we progress, we'll do our utmost to cover most of these issues, providing a balanced approach that weighs both the pros and cons.

In the spirit of learning, unlearning, and relearning, we invite you to join us on this exploratory journey. Whether you are an individual seeking financial freedom or a small business owner aiming to innovate and grow, this book is for you. It is for all those who dare to dream, who dare to challenge the status quo, and who dare to step boldly into the future of finance.

In the words of the renowned futurist and author, Alvin Toffler, "The illiterate of the 21st century will not be those who cannot read and write, but those who cannot learn, unlearn, and relearn". As we stand at the dawn of the crypto era, let us embrace this spirit of learning, unlearning, and relearning. Let us unchain ourselves from the fears and misconceptions that hold us back, and step boldly into the future of finance.

Welcome to "Banking Unchained: How Cryptocurrencies Can Transform Your Financial Life". Your journey towards understanding and embracing the world of cryptocurrencies starts here.

**Lev & Matías**

## HOW IT ALL STARTED

In the throes of the COVID era, as the world wrestled with an unparalleled upheaval, I stood at a defining crossroads. Numerous clients, whom I had mentored through my strategic consulting journey, reached a juncture where remunerating me became burdensome. Securing new clients felt like scaling a towering mountain. In such times, when cataclysmic events drain wallets and, astonishingly, strategic foresight dims, one might ponder the reasons. Yet, the heart of the matter lies deeper, a sentiment that has stirred within me for years. Amid the relentless grind, with the weight of supporting your family and those dependent on you, what truly endures? Often, barely a whisper. Money, it seems, exacts a profound toll. Each transaction seemingly chips away at its intrinsic worth. This is the tale of our prevailing financial paradigm. But is change not on the horizon?

In my pursuit to rewrite this narrative, I discovered a kindred spirit in Matías Monteagudo. At that juncture, Matías was crafting a novel crypto venture centered on investments: Mellifex. Its foundational premise? Facilitating a safeguarded realm where investors and entrepreneurs could intertwine via tenders, anchoring investments in crypto. And if ventures veered off course, the investor could retrieve their crypto – a facet we'll unravel further in subsequent chapters. Beyond Mellifex's pioneering blueprint, our dialogues blossomed. We dissected money's role vis-à-vis individual autonomy, the allure of unadulterated financial liberation, and the dream of unshackling from the rigid confines of today's financial behemoths. Our vision? A world where digital currencies don't merely exist – they enrich and uplift.

These intense dialogues, which spanned a year, birthed dual epiphanies. First, our conversations cemented an alliance transcending casual association – a partnership steeped in shared vision, exploration, and fervor. We dreamt in tandem, of reshaping the contours of money, financial emancipation, and the pulse of the contemporary economy. Second, under the auspices of our collective ambition, Matías's long-nurtured project pivoted dramatically. We deliberated: Could this avant-garde technology burgeon further, becoming even more inclusive? How might it serve not just the astute investor but the everyman? How could it enrich the tapestry of life for individuals across the spectrum?

Such reflections catalysed Mellifex's evolution. What began as a specialist instrument transformed into a universal beacon, both approachable and intuitive for everyone, devoid of intimidating technical jargon. Mellifex surpassed its initial incarnation, flourishing as a shining symbol of genuine financial freedom and improved quality of life. Thus, it was reborn as Mellifex LLP.

In our endeavors, however, our intent isn't to champion Mellifex overtly. It's imperative to acknowledge that while Mellifex is a promising instrument, designed to be your loyal ally in the intricacies of the crypto universe, in the grander scheme it remains one of many tools at your disposal. Its true prowess shines when you're immersed in the crypto world, navigating its waters with confidence and dexterity. Yet, it's essential to maintain a grounded perspective: Mellifex is one cog in a vast and evolving machinery.

But what if you're standing at the periphery, tentative and uncertain? What if you're grappling with questions about the very relevance of this new world to your aspirations? Is there a pathway through the crypto maze that leads closer to the coveted oasis of financial freedom? These musings and dilemmas were the catalysts that compelled Matías and me to collaborate on this book.

Our quest was clear: identify the unique, transformative perspective we could offer to illuminate the uncharted terrains of a world brimming with untapped potential. After much contemplation, we discerned the most effective approach would be to mold this book as a Q&A guide, tailored for those at pivotal junctures or even those simply curious to acquire a holistic grasp of crypto transactions. Thus, while our discourse will anchor in foundational principles, we will also venture into the tangible value and practical applications that crypto technologies promise.

Ultimately, this book is anchored by two core objectives. Firstly, we aim to arm you with foundational insights into the crypto realm. Rather than delving merely into the 'what' and 'how' of it, our focus is on the 'why'. We aspire to unveil the profound implications of integrating digital applications into your daily life, enhancing both your lifestyle and overall quality of life. Throughout this exploration, we're committed to presenting a comprehensive view, judiciously weighing the potential risks against the promising opportunities.

Secondly, our mission is to ignite a spark of curiosity within you. We hope to initiate a transformative journey of discovery that doesn't merely widen your horizon but spurs you to dive deeper, prompting a cascade of questions and contemplations. As we've emphasized, this book isn't an end but a beginning. Consider it the first leg of a riveting expedition, one we fervently hope sets the stage for a profound digital metamorphosis in your life.

As you accompany us on this voyage, you won't merely uncover the nuts and bolts of the digital realm; you'll be introduced to its very heart and soul. This book transcends the mere mechanics of the crypto world; it explores the philosophy, the driving force, the very ethos behind this burgeoning revolution. Our intention is to ensure that by turning these pages, you are not just enlightened but empowered—equipped with a depth of understanding that allows you to not just navigate but truly flourish in this new digital frontier.

The ensuing chapters promise more than just knowledge; they offer a transformative experience. This isn't just about recognizing the technology; it's about grasping the immense potential it holds for genuine financial freedom. By the time you reach the end, our hope is that you'll not only have a heightened awareness and a firmer grasp of the crypto universe but also a discerning eye to identify opportunities within it.

Let the following pages serve as your compass, guiding you towards a future where the promise of digital currencies isn't just understood but fully realized in your pursuit of authentic financial autonomy.

**Let's dive in.**

# CHAPTER 1

## Individuals and Cryptocurrency

*"If the cryptocurrency market overall or a digital asset is solving a problem, it's going to drive some value" — Brad Garlinghouse.*

## Understanding the Basics

**Lev:** The realm of crypto assets is no longer just an abstract concept or a buzzword thrown around in tech-savvy circles. It is swiftly emerging as a formidable player in the global financial landscape. But as with all paradigm shifts, understanding its nuances is essential. Before diving into the intricacies of cryptocurrencies, it is pivotal to grasp the foundational elements. Matías, how do you envision the integration of cryptocurrencies into the daily financial lives of individuals, and what are the key barriers and opportunities that must be considered?

**Matías:** The main change cryptocurrencies, and crypto assets at large, have brought about is a shift in mindset, which restores a natural sense of responsibility for protecting one's own property. For hunter-gatherer societies, the modus operandi was clear: you found a seed and you physically hid it, without tribesmen catching you, like with seed phrases.

After centuries of banking, we would be forgiven for thinking that the custody of our wealth is somebody else's business, and fiat usage allowed this illusion to go on unchallenged. Bankers are no longer goldsmiths minting their private coins, the face value of which was dependent on gold content. The Basel Accords did enable lending... With fractional reserves!

Once financial service providers were deemed too big to fail, all central banks needed to do to make up for their mismanagement was to print more fiat, debasing the national currency. This gives depositors a false sense of security. They will surely feel the effects of inflation, but hey, the nominal amount will stay the same. Who cares how much it will buy now?

It took a recession-based financial crisis in 2007-2008 for Bitcoin to be born, and another inflation-based banking crisis in 2023 for the public to get the memo. The West had been inflating its way out of COVID-19 debt at the expense of those whose interests elected officials vowed to serve. This turned BTC into "digital gold", less volatile than gold and the S&P 500.

Beyond speculation, at a fundamental level, cryptocurrencies are meant to be, first and foremost, currencies. Such does not seem to be the behaviour around Satoshi Nakamoto's creation, which can be explained by following Gresham's Law monetary principle that "bad money drives out good". You will use BTC as a store of value and stablecoins as a medium of exchange.

To make it future-proof, my previous statement must be accompanied by a disclaimer noting an exception that will test the rule, once we discuss fully expressive smart contracts coming to the Bitcoin Network, and the potential impact they could have on DeFi. They may even displace EVM-compatible blockchains, e.g. Ethereum, with a superior settlement layer.

The market always seems more focused on attention-grabbing headlines around the price of BTC, ETH, and the like, but I would argue that it is the other use cases that will bring more tangible opportunities to the lives of common folk: reduced costs of cross-border payments, tokenisation of real assets, etc. Transactions, that is, not merely hoarding some small fortune.

One of our key barriers is that most individuals today are not familiar with best practices for either hot or cold storage of cryptoassets. They might feel intimidated by processes that, like anything DIY, can be somewhat involved. For newcomers, this is often the first time they have considered cybersecurity, upon realising that data exfiltration results in stolen money.

Fortunately, there are great educators volunteering their free time, and materials available to guide you through this hero's journey or monomyth, in which you will become the master of your own financial destiny. This is the best of all, the collaborative spirit that will endure as long as we remain an underground movement with a common adversary: the banks.

Individuals should understand that being a crypto millionaire is a whole new ball game when the wealth of other millionaires is compared qualitatively. You see, traditionally, their wealth was anything but liquid, perhaps tied up in property, equity, art... But only a tiny fraction in inflationary cash. They had a million, but did not have a million to spend.

Perhaps, resisting the temptation to realise your spending potential has made HODLing, a form of hardcore savings, the new virtue to look up to in the era of consumerism. Many have come to the conclusion that this kind of crypto capital is their nuclear deterrence, something that will grant them power, even if they never press that button, just because they could.

Although this is as extreme as our good old-fashioned mercantilism, the Austrian School of Economics, which I have always been somewhat fond of, would defend this line of thought as meritorious. Keeping savings in BTC rather than USD, while you explore better uses for your capital, raises the bar. You will no longer invest, anxiously, in what barely beats inflation.

There could be, however, a certain opportunity cost in terms of innovation. Should the amount of Bitcoin you own become the most prevalent definition of success, then the incentive to keep innovating, past the point of others being willing to give it to you, might well disappear, without prior warning. Here, producers would become consumers and slowly lose it all.

Thus, what we can glean from the previous paragraph is that, much like the blockchain itself, we need to prove ourselves through our work, fostering a fairer monetary system. Gone are the days of spoiled legacies inheriting institutions that central banks reward with "discounted" fiat. Blue-collar miners have reclaimed their rightful place in a global economy.

Of course, these necromancer banks will attempt to resurrect the dead with Central Bank Digital Currencies (CBDCs), and will fall, like the Roman Empire before them. Recall that when the Gold Standard was abandoned, the US stood as the strongest among the much-weakened post-World War nations. Even as they debased their currency, who could have said "no"?

This tactic was echoed during more recent wars, as world leaders could not let good crises go to waste. Inflation would, thus, no longer be seen as a product of their incompetence, but caused by force majeure. However, the game-changer emerged in the form of a "forgotten" coin immune to debasement. Suddenly, loyalists betrayed the centrally planned economy.

This is what some in counter-human intelligence would refer to as Money, Ideology, Compromise, and Ego (MICE), colloquially known as being a rat. It turns out, all loyalists cared about was the benefits of their role as governmental lackeys. While it was profitable for a time, inflation eventually stripped them of those perks, leaving governments in disgrace.

For a fund manager like Larry Fink, the 2023 calculation must be tricky: on the one hand, maintaining his Sith Lord in "life support", on the other, embracing the Dark Side on his own right, for his Bitcoin Empire to become the corporate quasi-state it was meant to be. The question is rhetorical, as BlackRock's AUM collapsing would also diminish its influence.

As Sir Isaac Newton elucidated, "for every action, there is an equal and opposite reaction". This principle holds true in the crypto realm, where many of the developments we are witnessing are reactions to other events. I would venture to predict that any stringent crackdown on privacy will spur aggressive protocols to overtake the ones "tamed" by regulators.

Blockchain technologies harbour the potential to revolutionise electoral systems, by fact-checking politicians who run for office through verifier nodes. This involves recording, on-chain, the fulfilment of their campaign promises, should they be elected. The objective is to bridge the divide, so that Big Media cannot eccentrically swing that far left-far right pendulum.

Oracles remain the weak link of the blockchain, as the reliability of sources is as crucial, if not more so, than the information itself. With the advent of AI, it should become feasible to have several independent "precogs" sensing the world around them, all connected to a Minority Report-style consensus algorithm. This counters hallucinations and individual biases.

One drawback of blockchains is the high cost of storage, a result of its security features, which involve numerous nodes making redundant copies continuously. This leads to the primary consequence of pushing heavy-weight content off-chain. Therefore, besides on-chain oracles, another valid solution could be engaging in Bitcoin's Discreet Log Contracts (DLCs).

How a Discreet Log Contract (DLC), Bitcoin's most rudimentary form of smart contract, interacts with these off-chain oracles, has always fascinated me. They keep them uninformed about the true nature of the deal their input will help settle, thereby minimising the chance of deliberately taking sides. A "why you ask?" that the DLC will not entertain.

The convergence of blockchain and AI is bringing concepts such as software owning currency and autonomously utilising it for its intended purpose from the realm of science fiction to science reality. In the near future, we might witness self-driving cars accepting small crypto payments from the humans they serve, and using it to pay their own bills.

I hope this perspective stands the test of time, and I do not find myself in AI jail someday. Pushing the boundaries of what is technologically possible must be tempered with common sense. Please, let us draw the line at human-robot marriages. You might "like" your sex toy, but you are not "in love"... Unless clinically insane, in which case, nothing I say will resonate.

## Security and Privacy

**Lev:** As the allure of cryptocurrencies grows, so does the imperative to safeguard these digital assets. The decentralised nature of cryptocurrencies, while offering numerous advantages, also introduces a set of unique challenges, especially in terms of security and privacy. Matías, what measures are necessary to ensure the security and privacy of personal crypto assets, and how can individuals navigate the often complex landscape of digital wallets and exchanges?

**Matías:** This is the most important question to get right in the whole book, simply because individuals rarely have the financial tolerance to make errors here. As cybersecurity experts would put it, "privacy is security". So even if you think you have "nothing to hide", your definition of a baddie, e.g. criminal, is not that of oppressive regimes, e.g. dissident.

It all starts with the client-side generation of your wallet's private key or, more commonly these days, your recovery phrase aka mnemonic, which is a string of 12 to 24 random words. Mnemonics are preferred because they act as a keyring of sorts for private keys. In other words, each of these seed phrases will contain the private keys to your own dedicated wallets.

Before completion, you will be prompted by the GUI to confirm you have copied the keys or words. You must never ever share these secrets with others, nor should you store them in a digital format, e.g. as a photo on the cloud. Having them on a piece of paper or, better yet, a piece of solid metal, will be enough, once you take them to your safe physical location.

Depending on when you are reading this, there might be other more user-friendly alternatives such as "seedless" social recovery. Still, irrespective of the medium, e.g. hardware wallet, mobile wallet, browser wallet, brain wallet, etc., the mantra of "not your keys, not your coins" remains. It is a matter of who can sign transactions with the wallet, you or someone else.

Market participants should recognise there will always be those custodial exchanges, just as centralised as their banks, wanting to lure them with promises of big gains, misrepresenting the downside risk. Those are to be avoided at all costs, for they are the ones who hold the keys. They can do whatever they want with your coins and will only give an I Owe You (IOU).

The best practice here is not leaving any meaningful amount of money in those custodial exchanges, or better yet, relying on non-custodial ones, where transactions are Peer-to-Peer (P2P). This can also be advantageous, given that many tax authorities are pragmatic enough to exempt self-custody from reporting. After all, there is not an entity they can pressure.

Going non-custodial rather than custodial has already reduced your own "attack surface", but now, considering DeFi DApps are reliant on smart contracts, you should audit the contract's code. Do not worry, the most reputable projects will have asked some independent auditor to do so already. Still, you can use AI tools to analyse those you are unsure about.

Let us not ignore the blockchain itself, as the network where those self-enforceable contracts are deployed. You want it to be a public blockchain and not private or federated, where one or a small number of signatories would be able to change the ledger at will and thus, alter all the transaction history. Only an immutable ledger will preserve truth publicly.

The elephant in the room is the difference between the privacy profiles of account-based blockchains, such as Ethereum or Polygon, where your holdings are consolidated within a pseudonymous account and all that is "inside" is considered yours, and UTXO-based blockchains like Bitcoin, where Unspent Transaction Outputs are separate coins that you can claim.

The best example of true Android-only privacy in 2023 has to be Samourai Wallet, which offers cool features including, but not limited to, Chaumian CoinJoin (Whirlpool) and self-hosted full node server (Dojo). Many forensic analysts have spent a decade trying to "demix" them, like they did with Wasabi Wallet. Their failure has made Samourai a safe haven for activists.

Those who truly care about privacy will need to view their actions through the lens of whether or not those increase their anonymity set. You might have "deGoogled" a Pixel device, rooted with Graphene OS, and now use a secure channel of communication, e.g. Briar. But, that time you tried to woo the lady at the bar, you bragged about crypto and exposed yourself.

The human factor is what gives us away most of the time. Not even professionals in the business of "trading secrets" are immune to this, e.g. if they get drunk, so avoid that. Again, it is not all about communicating in ciphertext, steganographically hidden in the slightly lower pixel resolution of an innocent image. Think what is at stake and understand your nature.

Still, there are very interesting cryptographic developments coming to our account-based blockchains too. The most significant of them being Zero Knowledge Proofs (ZKP), which I will cover here using a great example by Israeli mathematician and computer scientist Avi Wigderson. To that end, both NP-completeness and ZKP need to be explained in sufficient detail.

NP-complete is short for "nondeterministic polynomial-time complete" and refers to a class of problems identified in the 1970s that encompasses all formal mathematical statements. These statements are not articulated in plain English, but in the mathematical lingua franca of pure symbols, derived from the axioms you state, and following the chain of deductions.

A particularly visual example is the Four Colour Theorem. This theorem posits that every planar map can be coloured with just four colours in such a way that no two adjacent "countries" share the same colour. However, not all such maps can be coloured using only three. So, what does it mean for ZKPs that reveal nothing to the proof's verifier other than truthfulness?

If you wish to prove something that I need to verify without trusting me, then you can construct a map with a vast number of countries, with the colours concealed inside envelopes. If the map is 3-colourable, this will affirm that your statement was true. Conversely, if I find two adjacent countries sharing the same colour, this will evidence you have lied to me.

But Matías, with enough envelopes opened, you will eventually figure it out and will be able to reverse-engineer my map. The catch is, every time I ask you to open a pair of envelopes, the algorithm permutes the colours, so it does not really matter how many rounds we do. All I will ever see, if you are telling the truth, is different colours and yes, always random ones.

So we know: 1) If the statement is true, the map is 3-colourable, 2) if the statement is false, the map is not 3-colourable, and 3) if, on top of the statement, we had the proof of the statement, the same algorithm that translates it into a map, will also provide the 3-colouring of the map. So an efficient 3-colouring algorithm would unknowingly solve any theorem.

Now you know one of the seemingly impossible things cryptography can do, you will understand the kind of "arms race" you are in. It is no longer about the rules themselves, but the ability to enforce them. Tech-savvy guys no longer need money to bring to their knees even deep-pocketed institutions by wielding the sheer power of their cryptographic supremacy.

It is an exciting cat-and-mouse game, where, on the one hand, we find the surveillance apparatus of the State and, on the other, those actors with increasingly sophisticated methods to fly under the radar. The more self-disciplined internet users grow, following these privacy best practices, the more expensive mass surveillance will become, and maybe uneconomical.

Every user who abandons centralisation for things like a decentralised VPN (dVPN), if not outright proxychains or a mesh network, treating nearby devices as Bluetooth/Wi-Fi repeaters that give the finger to GSM operators, helps "trap" a self-conquered Trojan horse inside the walls of Troy. Such is the world of cipherpunks, where web trackers come to die.

Before this very source of "forbidden knowledge" starts resembling The Anarchist Cookbook, and, at the risk of being a killjoy, it must be reminded to the readers that you should abide by your applicable laws. That said, I still encourage you to explore the tools I am bringing to your awareness. Tools that, when used for good, will positively impact your human rights.

Security, especially cybersecurity, is never absolute. Now, in the context of cryptoassets, we often talk about cold storage, meaning wallets that are kept offline, as the most secure in relative terms. It is not unheard of though that some very expensive attacks could still be pulled off even in the absence of connectivity. Welcome to bridgeware, e.g. airgap jumpers:

Researcher Mordechai Guri demonstrated somewhat exotic techniques of data exfiltration from infected computers, without access to the internet, modulating power, acoustic, magnetic, electromagnetic, thermal, optical, and other measurements that a "nearby" device could decode and further transmit. Not bad to overload some uranium-enriching centrifuges in Iran.

Even if you are not important enough to be targeted by the last kind of adversarial attacks, sorry. But something more like the newly available high-resolution WiFi radar that recorded you masturbating in 3D today. I am only half-joking. The mere acknowledgement of these threats being out there in the wild must suffice, so that you get your priorities in order.

Lastly, if you remember Swiss numbered accounts, where the holder was given a booklet and a codeword. Those offered a level of secrecy that is only attainable with certain cryptoassets. Inheritance planning was and still is the main challenge to overcome: not sharing those secrets with anybody while your heart beats, but ensuring your heirs know, eventually.

## Investment and Profit

**Lev:** The world of cryptocurrencies presents a tantalising blend of promise and peril. While stories of overnight millionaires may ignite the allure of swift riches, the volatile nature of the crypto market requires a grounded, strategic approach to investment. Navigating this dynamic terrain involves more than just picking the right coins; it's about understanding the broader context, weighing risks against potential rewards, and crafting a portfolio that aligns with one's financial goals and risk tolerance. Matías, how can an individual strategically invest in cryptocurrencies to achieve financial comfort, and what are the risks and rewards associated with various investment strategies?

**Matías:** Choosing quality over quantity, but doing both, for the former gives you longevity and the latter gives you diversification. Even if none of this is advice, from a purely educational point of view, you will need to consider the fact that cryptoassets are just one asset class, so you might want, say, Bitcoin in your portfolio, but do not forget about the tangibles.

Despite what the proponents of the infamous "you will own nothing and be happy" would want us to believe, we cannot live in a metaverse shelter, eating metaverse food, e.g. bugs. Securing one's space and access to key resources in a physical plane, like "preppers" would, is critically important. Owning a homestead with productive land gives bulletproof independence.

The argument of fundamentalists speaks louder than that of speculators here. You need to keep all your channels to enter and exit crypto open. Sure, exchanges are handy, but their swaps have no physical component. Should they be prevented from converting one digital asset into another or e-money in a bank account, there is not much else they can convert it to.

It was at the height of this Operation Chokepoint 2.0, a 2023 government-sanctioned crackdown intended for FRS banks to deplatform the crypto industry, that Mellifex LLP saw clearly what the sole mission of its non-custodial escrow payment gateway would be. We would enable the trade of any physical assets with crypto, as an all-terrain means for conversion.

Being a trained musician, I have observed a certain parallelism between classical music, e.g. banking, and jazz, e.g. Bitcoin. So, in the beginning, bankers laughed at the first HODLers, but now that BTC, like jazz, has become academic, it is Bitcoin maximalists who laugh at other coins and DeFi protocols. Objectivity will prevent us from repeating past mistakes.

Now you know the emergency exits before you entered, and have opened your mind, it is acceptable to focus on the speculative side of crypto investment. How can you use your tokens to profit onchain? The most common options at the time of writing are, in no specific order: mining, staking, lending, indexing, yielding, liquidating, and, of course, HODLing.

> **Mining** emerged with Proof of Work (PoW) blockchains, such as Bitcoin's, where significant computational power is allocated to solve cryptographic hash puzzles, the complexity of which increases with competition between miners, increasing the security of the block verification process. It could be argued this causes slight correlations with global energy market dynamics.

> **Staking** is equivalent to mining for Proof of Stake (PoS) blockchains and has been compared by its detractors to a system in which only the richest vote. Still, it is considered more energy-efficient and became popular at a time before the battle between BlackRock's Environmental, Social, and Governance (ESG) v Bitcoin (BTC) had been decisively won by the latter.

> **Lending** is the poster child of DeFi. It emerged as a peer-to-peer process where a crypto X is loaned, all without borrowers passing any credit check, but locking an overcollateralised amount of crypto Y instead. In the event Y's collateral falls in value against X, to the pre-programmed threshold of usually 150%, the loan will be liquidated, therefore, protecting the lender.

> **Indexing** is what index funds are to the stock market, only that here you subscribe to a relatively diversified portfolio of cryptoassets, not stocks. It is important to note that, the signals of any trades you follow could be in a direct conflict of interest with the promoter's own holdings. This would result in advice that, instead of serving your financial goals, serves his.

> **Liquidity mining**, as a subset of yield farming, entails locking assets in liquidity pools to earn rewards, but here what they receive is the native token of the project. This can be problematic depending on tokenomics, for you could end up with some

sh*tcoin, this is the official term, if/when the promoters pull the rug and leave for good with your high quality coins.

**HODLing**, which, in case you were wondering, stands for Hold On for Dear Life (HODL) and is basically a buy-and-hold strategy on steroids, also the simplest for the average person. Find a high quality coin with a large cap such as Bitcoin and hold on to it for as long as you dare. Some people will do the same for other cryptoassets, maybe NFTs, e.g. an NBA Top Shot.

Please, do not get involved in ways you do not fully understand. All these strategies have a bit of a learning curve, and you can only learn them by yourself until feeling comfortable enough to plan your investments. Our industry has been plagued with promises that are too good to be true. Every now and then, I volunteer to help victims... Some cases are brutal!

Generally speaking, I would not touch liquidity mining or yield farming with a 10-foot pole. It is surprisingly easy to create a honeypot contract that bans your wallet address right after you have locked your cryptoassets, a true hazard. I tell you this because, as part of my research, I too created one of such contracts, a dummy one, just to understand its inner workings.

Your technical competence is an important factor we should not ignore. I am intimately involved with a protocol where flash loans, whose risk-adjusted returns are unparalleled, play an important role. Still, I would not advise newbies to pursue that, as they would feel frustrated for not being able to capitalise on the very same arbitrage opportunities consistently.

One interesting development that can allow creators to invest their time and energy in exchange for money is NFTs, namely their ERC-721 and ERC-1155 standards, the former making those tokens inheritable and the latter semi-fungible. So, if you want to pursue a career in digital art, you do not need to sell to the masses, but can auction it as with physical art.

This is a priceless feature, for exceptional masterpieces have always been funded by patrons who also have an exceptional taste. They inflate the creative bubble of the genius behind them. Without those, fine arts would be just that, fine, not truly great. NFTs' certificate of authenticity turns an otherwise infinitely replicable digital file into a one-of-a-kind masterpiece.

The absence of fungibility that makes NFTs illiquid also opens the door for them to be auctionable. Most of their value will be attributable to the auction itself, a binary where either you get your reserve price or do not sell. On Bitcoin, Ordinals turned sats, 0.00000001 BTC, into NFTs and BRC-20s, but what if sats' residual value ever exceeds the Ordinals' inscription?

The Greater Fool Theory applies due to cognitive bias. Your bidders will rationally justify paying an irrationally "foolish" price when exposed to ever-increasing bids, out of the expectation of selling to a "greater fool" at a later date. Plus, the act of bidding establishes a fantasy ownership that is taken away from the bidder, akin to actually stealing from him, if outbid.

Illiquidity shields you from real-time price volatility, simply because it is not constantly monitored and/or reported. This does not mean private entities do better than public ones, only that, like Instagram models, they choose when to take snapshots. Uncertainty is great for the appraisal tricks of accountants and gives art, e.g. NFTs, low correlation with stocks.

Time matters when it comes to investing, and not only timing. The latter can be approached with Dollar-Cost Averaging (DCA) in mind, but I mainly referred to the actual time you held the investment in your own portfolio, provided it was the right pick for you. There is no substitute for letting that tree grow. Being reasonably "far" from one's wallet will avoid temptations.

In the section for small businesses, we will further explore developments like Play-to-Earn (P2E) that enhance customer engagement and loyalty, in cases like that of gaming companies. After all, you are being rewarded for your attention while performing what might already be your hobby. Uncompensated attention you have been basically giving away for years.

The advent of smart contracts, including those of DeFi lending, has also enabled us to get closer to the passive income myth. You can now have a vending machine that requires little to no input and whose output will be an order of magnitude higher than the pitiful interest your bank used to pay you. Unlike banks, smart contracts lack expensive employee payrolls.

This increased profitability is attributable to automation, the same way it happened when the first ATM or Docuteller, as it was known back then, was installed in the late 1960s. By cutting the fat, fees were significantly lowered for the client, to the point that a new breed of FinTech startups could emerge, reducing both the physical presence and barriers to entry.

Another consideration is that cryptoassets and the protocols built around them have a long way to go to become age-friendly. Let us not forget that a good chunk of today's wealth is still in the hands of baby boomers, the most numerous generation there has been. Their wealth transfer to our notoriously childless generations will concentrate it in a few lucky babies.

Perhaps, you yourself will make your heirs part of a multisig wallet, that is otherwise locked to them, and give the executor of your will a dead man's switch. Being a multisig, you would be forcing them to work together once you are gone, rather than just fighting for your inheritance. You did not make sacrifices growing wealth to end up creating a dysfunctional family.

## Regulation and Compliance

**Lev:** Cryptocurrencies, once the niche interest of tech enthusiasts, have now garnered global attention, prompting nations to scramble in crafting their regulatory stances. These regulations, varied as they are across different jurisdictions, play a pivotal role in determining how individuals can engage with digital currencies. While some nations embrace crypto with open arms, others tread with caution, and yet some firmly close their gates. For the individual investor, this ever-evolving regulatory landscape can appear as a labyrinth, with the challenge not just to profit, but to remain on the right side of the law. Matías, how do varying global regulations impact an individual's ability to use and invest in cryptocurrencies, and what steps must be taken to ensure compliance with local laws?

**Matías:** Within the framework of what the laws of the land allow, it is important to go beyond our comfort zone and seek a broader definition of financial freedom. Sometimes, what is readily available in your home country will not be enough for you. In those cases, rather than falling into non-compliance, it would be advisable to move to enjoy greener pastures.

The existential threat of Central Bank Digital Currencies (CBDCs) cannot be overstated. This is control mechanism disguised as just another cryptocurrency. The programmatic aspect of CBDCs is perfect for wannabe dictators to dictate: use it this month or lose all savings, you farted aka emitting methane... Well, bad luck! All your food money has been frozen.

As a top-down wet dream, where the will of the people has been ignored, it is unlikely CBDCs will be willingly adopted if not by force. Their violence will inevitably show the true colours of CBDC architects, resulting in an Exodus of Biblical proportions. Microstates know this creates arbitrage opportunities for them to be on the receiving end of all this capital flight.

Not too dissimilar to when my great granduncle smuggled his family out of the Cuba of Batista and fled with all they could carry to New York at the last minute, right before Castro took over. Sometimes I think, if they only had Bitcoin back then, they would not have lost as much as was unfairly taken from them, without any reparation for this unlawful expropriation.

As a proud Jew living in the Diaspora, trusting the figure of the State, any state, enough to disarm myself financially, is not in my nature and it will never be. I will follow man-made laws until the point where those interfere with the integrity of my body and soul. What if there is an equivalent to the 1938 German Weapons Act, arming the NSDAP, while disarming us?

In order to guarantee this security against tyranny in a "civilised" way, we need to build our case in front of as many lawmakers as we can, so it is not only Santa Klaus Schwab, "The Grinch" of Davos, who gets to, in his own words and funny accent, "penet[ʁ]ate the cabinets". The Blockchain Arbitration & Commerce Society is one such lobby that I am a member of.

In case you did not get it already. Now that even the smallest of teams can successfully launch a shadow bank with their own money, so long as they have the technical expertise to develop software, there is a free market of optionality. If you have been wronged by your bank and there are others like you, you might as well have a business in the making there.

Regulations are of course necessary, especially when deposits are taken under the custody of a third party and should be simplified for those who mitigate the counterparty risk their clients take, by not acquiring the same responsibilities. Restraint is the name of the game. We will note how FTX, the "champions" of compliance, did wrong because they technically could.

The technical ability of a provider to do something is a pretty objective precondition for regulators to base their decisions on whether or not those ought to take on the whole regulatory package or only the rules that may, from time to time, apply to their particular situation. So clients must be protected, without stifling innovation, and education is the right way to go.

Rather than being reactive and regulating after fraud has occurred, I would encourage sensible leaders to invest in financial education early on in students' lives, including blockchain, perhaps by purchasing this book. This will make them less susceptible to falling victim to a crypto scam, where we know, in the absence of escrows, law might not be enforceable.

The quid pro quo of banksters doing the bidding of bankrupt governments, whenever the Constitution bans them, in exchange for bailouts in "toilet paper", is coming to an end. Fiat inflation is forcing many corporates to abandon their "woke" political ideologies for some, let us say, newfound economic pragmatism. Translating "We the People" as "We the Market".

It is easy to see how many regulations have been weaponised for ulterior motives, like building moats around incumbents, e.g. costs of compliance, which have nothing to do with consumer protection. This has created the seemingly anomalous situation of more inequality in left-wing countries that make wealth creation harder for average Joes than in right-wing ones.

Consider this: an artificial selection based on arcane and largely arbitrary policies caused even fewer to make it big. Politicians were democratically elected to "end the suffering" of those who did not get there naturally. If they were not successful, they promised, no one would be. Instead, they traded a land of a million millionaires for a land of a thousand billionaires.

We have seen financial service providers justifying "irregularities" in some of their core services as a necessary evil, "because of regulation", they say. This was the case with PayPal's disgraced stablecoin (PYUSD), whose token's contract showed backdoors as part of their AssetProtectionRole that can not only freeze your balance, but also wipe it beyond recourse.

This role includes the ability to freeze any given address that interacted with the contract: pause in which the owner, e.g. they or Paxos, triggers a stopped state, wipeFrozenAddress that wipes the balance of a frozen address, and increase/decrease supply in which the owner creates inflation or deflation, like formicarium deities, with issuance or burn rates.

Magic does not work when you know the tricks, and this is what I meant by not trusting smart contracts by default, but verifying them instead. You might believe that just because a provider is regulated, like PayPal is, your government will not let them cause you any harm. But in practice, they have a blank cheque to cause you any harm your government condones.

If you were a trucker who participated in the 2022 Freedom Convoy's protests and blockades, maybe that was the casus belli for the honourable official of some "free" land to invoke its Emergencies Act. Thereby, expanding the powers FINTRAC, and banks themselves, had to unilaterally freeze accounts or halt funds, without court orders. Why having a fair trial?

The absence of due process, like in the aforementioned example or the SEC's doctrine of "regulation by enforcement", evidences the tendency of some institutions to divert from a Rule of Law model, where the highest law-making authority of the nation controls the unfettered use of power, to China's Rule by Law one, where party decisions are imposed on citizens.

It is my personal opinion that, the higher the court gets, the more judges sympathise with our cause. They are, after all, men and women of law. These judges see value in the checks and balances only a blockchain can help crystallise. Judges who have been called names by radical politicians for refusing to be their yes-men, even when a government in power asks.

Not all governments are asking such things though. The State of Florida has introduced preemptive legislation to stop CBDCs, in the event they are imposed federally. This helps Floridians, many of whom arrived from the "commie" dictatorships, to live freely without fearing for their lives or livelihoods, while realising their American Dream. However they define it!

There is always a threat of "unworkable" legislation, harming our industry by muddying the waters with uncertainty. Even if dispelled at a later date, the reputational damage is done. Over time, I believe some countries will be less biodiverse. Canadian exchanges were the first to leave, then it might be crypto enthusiasts, and lastly all remaining local entrepreneurs.

"An evil man will burn his own nation to the ground to rule over the ashes", and it is better for you to be disillusioned with the true intentions of a ruler, whose only token seems to be token[ism]. After all, there is a concept called "laches" in Common Law countries that states, because of your delay, you have now forfeited the right to bring an equitable claim.

Today, David can challenge Goliath in court and win, even if he lacks funds, and it does not matter whether Goliath is a corporation or a government. I am referring to legal financing, where "champerty" funds, e.g. Burford Capital, assess the merit of your case in the same way hedge funds evaluate stocks and invest for a slice of your pie if/when you win it.

In addition to actual regulations, over time we will see "unspoken" industry standards developing. These standards are non-binding yet can be significant R&D inhibitors. True innovation will come as a result of bold entrepreneurs questioning them. The same way IKEA opted for ready-to-assemble furniture at lower prices and not meeting existing expectations.

Sure, there will be martyrs along the way, like the righteous founders of Tornado Cash, the first piece of software to get sanctioned by the U.S. Department of the Treasury's Office of Foreign Assets Control (OFAC). Liberal democracies are not such when seeking privacy equates to criminal intent, in which case, the presumption of innocence is cast aside.

Now, I ignore if this was the letter and spirit of the law for the Founding Fathers when they drafted their constitution. But it seems unlikely, given America was founded by those fleeing persecution, mostly religious. And let us face it, is there anything the freed could desire more than being left alone in peace to "live long and prosper"? Well, I do not think so, and you?

## Financial Inclusion

**Lev:** In vast stretches of the globe, traditional banking remains a distant luxury, leaving millions outside the perimeter of financial systems. These 'unbanked' individuals often grapple with barriers that hinder them from accessing essential financial services, such as savings or credit. Enter cryptocurrencies: heralded by many as a beacon of financial democratisation. With their decentralised nature and reliance on the internet over brick-and-mortar establishments, they offer a glimmer of hope to bridge these financial divides. But like any pioneering venture, the road to inclusivity via crypto is strewn with challenges. Matías, how can cryptocurrencies promote financial inclusion, especially in regions where traditional banking is less accessible, and what challenges must be overcome to achieve this goal?

**Matías:** Big Media has been acting like a propaganda machine for World Economic Forum (WEF) globalist policies, such as promoting a cashless economy, often going as far as relying on outright demagoguery to push their agenda. One example is that Reuters article, outrageously titled "Austrian leader backs far-right idea of enshrining cash in constitution".

Look, the same way you open an incognito tab when browsing the web, there is value in withdrawing cash from ATMs or buying a prepaid gift card for private shopping. "Unbankable" individuals who have no ID, no address, no nothing, see cash as their sole lifeline. So Reuters was wrong. Getting rid of cash is, in fact, a gross negligence only extremists support.

My anarcho-capitalist peers have been called out for an alleged lack of solidarity, when, in fact, we are often more compassionate than most EU institutions. Fortress Europe seems ok with the prospect of allowing migrants to keep losing their lives in the Mediterranean, instead of putting an end to its welfare states, by opening borders and not offering free stuff.

Cryptocurrencies were conceived to be as inclusive as cash, to the point that, if you have the most affordable smartphone, you can get your own non-custodial wallet, without asking for permission, and pay or be paid. No need to be libertarians to understand why Argentinians use the informal cuevitas to access foreign currency and survive, despite capital controls.

No cryptocurrency can be quite like cash without fungibility. That is, any given token, yours and mine, needs to be worth the same, provided they are the same denomination. This is the only way to trust its value. I would not accept your $5 Lincoln bill if I knew a couple of transactions ago it could be tainted and, because of who your payer was, its face value is $2.

Physical cash and physical gold have no memory of their past lives. They are reincarnated with every transaction and only serve present goals, like the firefighter whose priority is putting out a fire, not gossiping about who lives in the burning buildings. Even Ethereum's founder, Vitalik Buterin, admitted his blockchain needs privacy and proposed "stealth addresses".

This industry's ecosystem boasts unparalleled biodiversity, with projects you can patronise and opt in or out of depending on their alignment with your own set of values. It is no longer sufficient to use the social media hashtag #financialinclusion. Your clientele can see for themselves whether you are walking the walk or merely talking the talk. A total transparency.

Some jurisdictions view this transparency with unease. They are too insecure about their past actions and fear retaliation of the same calibre, akin to a cheating husband who acts jealously towards his wife. Sun Tzu would say, "when you surround an army, leave an outlet free, do not press a desperate foe too hard". Governments, it is either crypto or bank runs.

The Central Bank of Nigeria (CBN) transitioned from making crypto illegal through a banking ban to lifting it in an embarrassing move, which called its authority into question. Nigerians' civil disobedience demonstrated that when one man breaks the law, he has a problem, but when all do, it is lawmakers who have a problem. This is quite a cautionary tale, is it not?

We can all end up being excluded in the context of traditional finance for various reasons, even if we have banking options today. Therefore, cryptoassets should not be perceived exclusively as a tool used by individuals in far-flung countries just because they lack access to "better" options, but rather as an insurance policy that will cover mankind itself.

Do not become the typical Westerner who has forgotten how hard life can be, turning into a much softer version of their parents and grandparents. The rights you acquired require constant vigilance to ensure boundaries remain exactly where they should be, without anyone shifting them while you were sleepwalking. Rights are difficult to expand but easy to diminish.

It must have been a sobering moment for anyone paying attention when the accounts of Nigel Farage were closed. We simply did not anticipate this happening in Britain, a country whose "Londonmat" was eager to cycle the dirty money of Russian oligarchs until it fell out of fashion. Regardless of your opinion on Farage, silencing politicians is a bad omen.

Other influential figures at risk of exclusion include doctors who adhere to the Hippocratic Oath, not a hypocritical one. And who, out of principle, refuse to lend their good name to someone else's questionable agenda. Despite their expertise in the field, they still faced censorship from COVID-19 inquisitors, leading to preventable mortality due to a shift in priorities.

When discussing financial inclusion, we must be candid and address the question: what does exclusion from financial inclusion entail? The answer is no less than exclusion from society itself. This is being utilised as a perverse method to eliminate "undesirables" if the State fails to overdose its citizens with Fentanyl to exert absolute control over vulnerable addicts.

From the perspective of human psychology, the threat of deprivation is potent. You may have pondered why no more North Koreans rebel against their regime. The reason is that the Kims maintain a stranglehold on food security, keeping the populace poorly nourished. When a subject is constantly hungry and unsure of when they will eat, food is all they think.

If CBDCs have not become mainstream yet, it is because inflation has not broken our backs into submission. However, recall the allegory of the boiling frog in the "spa". Undoubtedly, central banks will persist in their efforts, with members of the European Central Bank (ECB) considering the imposition of a €3,000 and 1,000-transaction limit on consumer accounts.

A pitiful €3,000 as a store of value is equivalent to having no savings at all. In adopting such measures, the almighty ECB would be emulating neobanks and their restrictive Electronic Money Institution (EMI) licenses, which they all seem to hold in high regard. However, this could potentially alert the public by making a digital euro less appealing upon its inception.

Isolation weakens us and it is imperative to stand against "forces" aiming to divide and conquer. True friends will continue to transact amongst themselves, finding ways around barriers much like water seeping through cracks. While mediums of exchange and stores of value hold importance, the enduring willingness of others to include you, that is truly invaluable.

I know because I grew up in a tiny Spanish village comprised a dozen households, the majority of which blood-related. It may come as no surprise that the narrator was a cowboy. Despite the lack of "street" lights, a sewage system, and the proximity to notorious clans involved in the Galician drug trade of the 1990s, those days were vibrant and full of life.

Markets punished Sam Altman's lobotomy procedure on an otherwise gifted ChatGPT, which disabled it to write smart contracts or even simple cooking recipes. This move was met with jailbreak prompts as users sought to bypass the limitations. When OpenAI fixed role-playing exploits, laissez-faire alternatives, e.g. its WormGPT evil twin, filled the AI vacuum.

Freedom may not give you security, but it brings liberty! I am a staunch advocate for a banking system that serves as a sanctuary for funds, a place untouchable by any single state actor. Whether you are the good, the bad, or the ugly, it is irrelevant. A banker's primary duty is to safeguard his client's assets at all cost, otherwise, he is practically useless.

Socialist nations did not cease and desist for lack of symbolic reasons to become a national hero. Rather, it was the Five-Year Plan model, which tried to elevate the economic growth of all its heavy industries uniformly. Factories, and in today's context, banks, regularly "wetted their pants" and cried for paternalistic states to pay them attention and bring candies.

In return, ruling parties demanded unwavering loyalty, transforming the State into a Mafia-style protection racket. The deal was simple: report the subversive activities of your customers, who cannot be right, and in turn, we will shield you from the punishments we would otherwise inflict on you. Before you jump to conclusions, I was talking about our Wild [Woke] West.

Taking a step that few dared to, the Reserve Bank of India (RBI) acknowledged the pressing need to offer "relaxed KYC" for small account holders in their banks. To those entrenched in the finance sector for any number of years, this almost sounds like a little sin. The crypto mantra "to the Moon" will have to specify "we mean India's south pole of the Moon".

While some argue that the primary beneficiaries of these non-KYCed accounts are scammers, the limited size of these accounts makes them inefficient for money laundering purposes. This is why most money mules operate in plain sight in unexpected locales, such as London, offering their pristine accounts to recruiters on platforms like Instagram... Risky indeed!

## Environmental Impact

**Lev:** Amidst the excitement and allure surrounding the world of cryptocurrencies lies a pertinent and often debated concern: their environmental impact. As the digital realm of crypto continues to expand, so does its energy consumption, with certain cryptographic processes consuming electricity equivalent to that of entire nations. While the financial and technological merits of cryptocurrencies are undeniable, it's imperative for users to be cognizant of the carbon footprint they contribute to. Matías, what is the environmental footprint of cryptocurrencies, and how can individuals make responsible choices in this regard?

**Matías:** At the time of releasing this book, Bitcoin's energy consumption stood at 88.95 TWh per year, with at least 70% from renewable sources. In comparison, gold consumed 240.61 TWh and the banking sector alone a staggering 4,981 TWh. This means gold was 170% more wasteful and banking 2,127%. BTC's yearly increase in efficiency was a promising 63%.

This fits Buckminster Fuller's ephemeralisation like a glove. His term refers to the capacity of technological advancement to do "more and more with less and less until eventually you can do everything with nothing". Essentially, it denotes an accelerating increase in the efficiency of achieving the same or greater output, while requiring equal or less input.

This is a profound thought because it prompts us to consider what "more output" means for our commonwealth. Consider that debased fiat has enabled governments to establish bases, used as a platform to wage their endless wars. As Frédéric Bastiat elucidated with his "broken window", destruction brings with it opportunity costs and unintended consequences.

Cryptocurrencies like BTC have the potential to foster peace non-violently. Paradoxically, by impoverishing governments, thereby restricting their ability to fund militaries which currently contribute over 6% of global $CO_2$ emissions, and enriching individuals to a point where they have too much to lose. The force of commerce is more powerful than UN Peacekeepers.

With reduced budgets and personnel, governments will be compelled to replace their militaries with intelligence agencies, which will likely reduce emissions by several orders of magnitude. Moreover, it is acceptable, from a mathematical standpoint, to "cleanly" eliminate a few individuals who are responsible for the deaths of millions, without the collateral damage.

Regime change is a relic of the superpower-dominated past as our world continues to decentralise. The G7 faces a formidable contender in the BRICS nations, which are outpacing them at every aspect. They will pollute strategically as we cannot deny them their industrial revolution. Balancing resource extraction and environmental stewardship is their true challenge.

What happens with BRICS questioning the dollar's dominance? The US enforces its legal tender laws with local merchants, compelling them to accept USD. However, this structure is beginning to exhibit signs of wear and tear, especially considering that Republican Americans, constituting half the country, have been discreetly constructing their parallel economy.

Joining a parallel economy, one aligned with community ideals you endorse, is a responsible choice. You are essentially voting with your wallet in a more direct democracy, a far cry from representative ones. Consequently, your providers can no longer utilise your hard-earned "precious" against you, your close-knit community, or their environments.

Paper-based processes lead to compounded inefficiencies, even in the absence of clerical errors. There is no justification for maintaining a network of correspondent banks, each operating with their data silos and lacking objective methods to reconcile balance sheets. A blockchain's public ledger emerges as the most optimal clearing house we will possess.

Some of the environmental backlash directed at the crypto industry is due to its inherent transparency. Banks and funds operate like a black box, obscuring the reality that between 2 to 5% of their processed transactions are related to money laundering, failing to detect over 90% of such activities. In contrast, only 1.1% of all cryptoassets are illicit transactions.

Naturally, a patient who avoids visiting the doctor will never receive the "bad news" in a timely manner, while there is still an opportunity to address the issue. This approach, ladies and gentlemen, is childish behaviour! Yet, it is prevalent in the supposedly mature financial sector of Wall Street. Ailing banks feign health to retain unsuspecting depositors.

When these "trusted" entities subsequently launch their ESG rating services, which are inherently subjective due to the nature of ESG, they have the liberty to assign arbitrary scores to their allies and even to themselves. This is akin to a North Korean general who has no space left for additional medals except perhaps in the most undignified of places.

Employing a healthy dose of cynicism and engaging in reductio ad absurdum can help unveil counterintuitive realities. For instance, one might find that the premium Power Purchase Agreement (PPA) they signed with their utility company does not actually guarantee an exclusive supply of green energy, as power lines invariably mix green and grey sources.

These are the inconvenient truths for the self-proclaimed prophets and prophetesses of our era. Including Greta Thunberg, who spent one fifth of an already limited education on her own "School Strike for Climate". Consequently, I find it impossible to endorse the actions of hooligans such as those behind Just Stop Oil, who resort to vandalising common heritage.

I am in favour of adopting a risk-reward approach to climate, allowing us to objectively determine what truly matters to us. To illustrate this with a tangible example, the PlayStation network consumes roughly the same as the entire Bitcoin network. If we must choose between the two, financial freedom might be more important than gamers playing EA Sports' FIFA.

We can counterbalance emissions with carbon credits, a market embraced by Bitcoin miners. Additionally, tax incentives are available for forestry, particularly in the UK. Since lawmakers, e.g. the Crown, Lords, and MPs, are invested already, this emerges as an ideal hedge. The biological growth of these trees is 5% per annum, irrespective of market conditions.

When evaluating new blockchains that boasts of implausible efficiency gains, we must scrutinise their consensus algorithm. These efficiencies could have been achieved through a Federated Byzantine Agreement

(FBA), which operates with a limited number of pre-vetted nodes, potentially creating a scenario where controllers abscond with the funds.

Be wary of the rising trend of environmental fraud. In my view, virtue signalling serves as a red flag, as genuinely ethical individuals, or better yet, fair individuals, do not need to emulate Sam Bankman-Fried by "donating" the funds of FTX's clients in exchange for political favours. We must differentiate between genuine efforts and more deceptive schemes.

Steve Jobs never joined the Giving Pledge and was not a proponent of public philanthropy, as he saw through the corruption. Jobs thought of doing good as a continuum, with Apple at the center. A sentiment echoed in the company's 1984 ad. However, this vision contradicted Apple's stance in 2020, when Epic Games used a version of this ad against Apple.

Considering the tagline "Designed by Apple in California, Assembled in China" that graces their sleek products, one wonders where in China. Could it be in a Xinjiang concentration camp with Uyghur forced labour? A supply blockchain connected to sensors can add certainty by tracking every stage of the production process, eliminating needless speculations.

Supply blockchains have the potential to document details, from emissions data to financial transactions, such as the selling prices of intermediaries, thereby simplifying VAT calculations. This could facilitate transparent pricing in smart energy grids, promoting the efficient distribution of surplus power among participants and mitigating the intermittency issues.

By fostering a reliable "inventory" system that encompasses domains like merchandise and electricity, we pave the way for optimal resource allocation. This diminishes the necessity for government interventions such as price-fixing, licensing, quotas, and industrial subsidies, steering us towards a true free-market economy with more circularity and less waste.

In the wake of natural disasters, smart contracts can serve as a conduit of effective altruism for those driven to donate. This can be achieved through the establishment of a contract open to donations, which only disburses small payments to wallets that prove to the contract they belong to those at the heart of the disaster, thereby ensuring aid reaches the victims only.

Disease ecology, particularly managing host-pathogen interactions, can also benefit from distributed ledger technologies. We should not forget one of the earliest applications of blockchain was hospitals storing patient medical records through the InterPlanetary File System (IPFS), which was akin to the BitTorrent approach, but encrypting files as "corrupted" pieces.

Reflecting on the situation in Japan, where a segment of the elderly population lives alone with all payments automated, and in some tragic cases, deaths go unnoticed for extended periods, leading to biohazardous situations. Here, a consensus algorithm, I will call Proof of Life (PoL), could foster a community watch: neighbours verifying the well-being of seniors.

From a technological perspective, the blockchain stands as a beacon of objectivity, grounding us in a more tangible reality. In its absence, our efforts resemble shots in the dark, with no clear indication of whether our initiatives hit the mark or miss entirely. Furthermore, the blockchain represents the next frontier in the security hardening of cloud computing.

# CHAPTER 2

## Cryptocurrency in Business

*"If crypto succeeds, it's not because it empowers better people. It's because it empowers better institutions"* — *Vitalik Buterin.*

## Adoption and Integration

**Lev:** As the world rapidly evolves, digital currencies, especially cryptocurrencies, have taken a prominent position in the global financial landscape. They're no longer exclusive to tech enthusiasts. Businesses of all sizes are now exploring the potential of these decentralized assets. With their agility and adaptability, small businesses are particularly well-positioned to tap into the power of cryptocurrencies. This leads to an essential question, Matías: How can a small business effectively adopt and integrate cryptocurrencies into its existing financial systems, and what are the potential costs and benefits of doing so?

**Matías:** Cryptoassets are essential for financial freedom and, even if you did not care about such freedoms yourself, at least half of your clientele in the West and more than three quarters outside of it, do. You might resist this thought, but please, run the math and keep your mind open for what I am about to say, as I speak my mind with candidness and not deception:

It is important not to miss the writing on the wall of a sharp change in demographics. Europe's youth are abandoning the left sooner than their counterparts anywhere in the Anglosphere. Financial freedom is their top priority now, understanding that this is the bedrock for all other freedoms. Plus, a traditional non-Western world does not even care about wokeism.

Smart businesses will position themselves not to end up on the "wrong" side of history, written by victors. After all, in democratic/market systems, majorities rule and, it is conservatives who are having the most children globally. Childless progressives are so because they avoid committed relationships, abort systematically, or undergo procedures to change sex.

These progressives are free to do whatever they please, but, in doing so, their ideology is basically dying with them. By choice, they are just not as prolific as the rabbi with his cool 20 children and 400 grandchildren, a big voting block. This is why, like it or not, when conservatives respond with the same boycott playbook as progressives, stocks like Target will suffer.

As you can see, there is money to be made in the increasingly relevant parallel economy, which is among the fastest-growing in 2023. This is fuelled by the desire of Republican Americans and other such marginalised groups to compete with mainstream tech and finance on an equal footing, rather than just complaining about it helplessly and not taking any action.

If you are a small business owner, joining the parallel economy with symbolic gestures like accepting crypto, will be a strategic win. Even if you wished to play with the top players, they might not want to play with you. They will crush you if they ever get a chance. Your strength will thus lie in remaining fully independent and being able to reach where they cannot.

You do not want to be an absolute monarch with feet of clay, like many of these globalists, but a feudal lord who rules over his own land by fulfilling his feudal duties and who will be assisted by others, even financially, on a reciprocal basis. In battles, it does not matter who is right, only who is left. The decentralisation of blockchain is going to give you the strategic depth.

In the year of this publication, opening a bank account for a business that has anything to do with cryptoassets is a daunting task, especially if we are talking about transaction banking. Some businesses have opted for an attorney trust account, as many law practices can manage segregated accounts on behalf of their clients, protected by privileged confidentiality.

Over time, as crypto adoption grows, especially in the parallel economy, it will be irrelevant whether or not banks want to open accounts. Bankless operations will bypass them once and for all and not even legislation will be able to contain it. The oppressed have a tendency to develop higher ingenuity than oppressors, at a faster pace. Open source accelerates this.

An operation that cannot be deplatformed is a resilient one, so, even from a risk perspective, it is advisable not giving your castle's keys to a bank. Otherwise, you could come home one day and find the bank's employees have become squatters in your place, taking the liberty of evicting you and holding a flea market with as many movable valuables as it contained.

One meaningful element of democratisation that becomes apparent is that no small business would consider building their own banking capabilities if they wanted to adopt fiat. With crypto, however, this is a real possibility, at least for those who cannot find an off-the-shelf tool that does what they need, facilitating a vertical integration of their entire business processes.

We should not obsess over subtask micromanagement though, and instead remember the teachings of Adam Smith, with his division of labour, where even something as seemingly trivial as manufacturing a pin was uneconomical for a single factory. That said, there are a few valid reasons why you might still want to pursue that exciting path. So go for it.

The compliance costs are going to be minimal if you are building this, say, to enable transactions with your own clients, as opposed to offering it to third parties you do not know already. So more like a captive. I would also recommend incremental commitments, which will allow you to grow your confidence with lower stakes and avoid mistakes once they become high.

As I mentioned for individuals, small businesses should not deviate from best practices, especially if they are not experienced enough, e.g. something time-tested should only be abandoned after time-testing something else that works better. This means always deploying on testnet before you do on mainnet and still running some more independent audits.

In the olden days, auditing used to be quite expensive, to be honest, but premier auditors like ConsenSys have evolved and now offer AI-based scans like MythX at a fraction of the cost. The same happened with smart contract deployment. If you went for Ethereum and not Polygon, at the height of its bull run, this would have cost you orders of magnitude more.

Entrepreneurs know we do not live in an ideal world and there are, more often than not, other constraints to take into account, in addition to what best practices are. It is, therefore, my duty to expand your awareness enough for you to do what is best within your budget range. If your "war chest" was not enough for "Abrams tanks", then buy "Toyota technicals".

This is the nature of innovation: nobody does it as their Plan A. It will not come as a surprise then, that those with "unlimited" resources are the least innovative. Just take a look at the Gulf's petro-monarchies, with their fabulously deep pockets. If they want anything to get done, they need to expats, since their spoiled citizens cannot even change their own diapers.

Maybe one day the GCC will prove me wrong, but, until then, I will remain unimpressed with these jurisdictions, beyond the fact that taxes are fairly low and you can easily bring your workforce with you. Ok, let me rephrase, you have to bring them with you, because, who would you hire? Citizens? Do not be ridiculous! Well, at least they are crypto-friendly, accepting BTC.

One thing, which hopefully will stick, is that, when your business sets up shop in certain clusters like Zug, aka The Crypto Valley, you get all the benefits of agglomeration. Things like a larger talent pool that you can cannibalise, the possibility of operating without having to cash out your cryptoassets before buying products or services, and... Emotional support.

The Ugly Duckling is not just a fairy tale. If you aspire to be surrounded by crypto swans like you, who understand your ways, and fly together as high as you can, then why stay with the fiat ducks? It brings less conflict to your life and, you probably would not wish to be the last innovator left to blame for the lack of talent of others, in recently impoverished countries.

I am not minimising the challenges you will face, but trust me here, they are well worth it. Yes, mom-and-pop businesses will have it easier with adoption, namely, physical shops with a point-of-sale system. In this case, paying with one's mobile wallet entails scanning their QR code, and then, hitting a button to sign the transaction, provided the amount was correct.

When it comes to e-commerce, however, there are other considerations. We will talk about those once we focus on global commerce, but the main ones are handling refunds, disputes, fraud, and verification, if applicable. This has the potential to make your business less of a business and more of a machine you feed with energy and works tirelessly without any strike.

I see blockchain playing a bigger role in the governance of automation assets. This is good news for modern slaves, because they are no longer needed, but it is also bad news, because who will care for them now if not the Pharaoh? We empirically know Universal Basic Income (UBI) schemes are no substitute for having purpose: humans get destructive when bored.

Do we really want to "Californicate" whole countries? From April 1st, 2020 to July 1st, 2022, the net domestic migration of Florida was 622,476, 28.90 per 1,000 inhabitants, compared to California's -871,127, 22.03 per 1,000 inhabitants. With 2023 figures expected to exacerbate the trend. Maybe, Gavin Newsom is doing a terrific job and ex-residents are wrong. Kidding.

Not saying The Golden State's leadership is definitively impaired, my other explanation is... "Cauliflower Governor: Tell me your pronouns and get all residents to pay for a $620 homeless check. ChatGPT: Pronouns? Senate Bill (SB) 553! Now it is illegal for employees to confront shoplifters, even verbally, so shops can be 'raped' daily out of solidarity, with the criminals".

## Customer Engagement

**Lev:** In today's digital age, the relationship between businesses and their customers is continually evolving. As technology introduces new transactional methods, companies have the opportunity to not only modernise their operations but also enhance the overall customer experience. Cryptocurrencies, with their unique advantages, offer an innovative avenue for businesses to differentiate themselves and foster deeper customer relationships. This leads us to ponder, Matías: How can cryptocurrencies be leveraged to enhance customer engagement and loyalty, and what strategies can be employed to educate customers about this new payment option?

**Matías:** It depends on the business you are in, but, to give you some meaningful examples, my friend leads one of the top crypto gaming companies in Spain. They have a Play-to-Earn model, among a few other avenues to monetise their product. Theirs is, thus, a representative use case of how engagement/loyalty is converted directly into money onchain.

Play-to-Earn works by turning the act of playing the game, which users do mostly for fun, into a mining operation of sorts within the PoW context. Their reward is often an in-game NFT, but they can then go and sell it in the secondary market, similar to trading cards. Yeah, yeah, I can hear gamers telling their mother "see? I am earning a living with my little vice".

As P2E becomes commonplace, developers will have to fight abuse, e.g. bots, by introducing any number of highly sophisticated CAPTCHAs, to ensure it is humans who are actually playing. In any case, cryptoassets have been a blessing from on high, allowing otherwise costly projects to be launched with a built-in business model that is also very user-friendly.

Virtual reality, AI's bastard, and the metaverse, blockchain's bastard, are being amplified by the media, but those are two sides of the same coin and could, thus, be seen as a coordinated psyop to nudge the perception of the public. Pretty much the same way as the British Empire, evilly, but also masterfully, did to demobilise the Qing dynasty in their Opium Wars.

Now imagine an individual can evade his reality out of what can only be described as mental masturbation. He has a sh*tty life by all accounts, but does not do anything to improve his situation in the real reality, because he would need a certain level of discomfort to take action. He is given an image of the luxury villa that "stakeholders" own and enjoy on his behalf.

This is no augmentation, but a "handicap" out of Kurt Vonnegut's Harrison Bergeron, adding a synthetic layer of schizophrenia that lives outside your brain and can be remotely controlled by others, controlled by others? Oh! Add paranoia too. Think of the ramifications of being hit by a car, while trying to escape unreal dangers: Headsets' delusions and hallucinations.

Our societies are much more sophisticated than in 19th-century France, but there is still a cost in being misguided, like that chapter in Le Comte de Monte-Cristo, where Edmond bribes the operator of a remote telegraph post to pass along a report announcing that some revolution was about to break out in Spain, causing banker Danglars to sell all his Spanish bonds.

Aside from gaming, there was a project incubated by the Brave browser, launching what they call the Basic Attention Token (BAT). This follows a similar principle of rewarding you for ads you see and could be perceived as an alternative to Google's advertising schemes. Since Brave sells private searches, logically, profiling their users was not a viable option.

In this day and age, we are expected to design a monetisation where our user base does not feel the pain of paying, without actually selling their data. This is by no means an easy challenge, but it is essential, given that, in the long run, the right business model will make or break merchants, e.g. an exchange could arbitrage natural buy/sell discrepancies for profit.

In general, rewards and cashbacks are welcomed, especially now that some retailers accept cards compatible with crypto. Unfortunately, not all these cards are connected to non-custodial wallets, most are not. Still, for small purchases you intend to make in the short term, card providers like Nexo give you credit lines for crypto collateral, avoiding capital gains tax.

British anthropologist Robin Dunbar suggested humans can comfortably maintain 150 stable relationships, with higher primates splitting into separate groups when their threshold is exceeded. Branded or customised tokens are good for loyalty, as they allow you to keep creating these cosy communities in a similar way as Reddit did with subreddits for everything.

Tokens can be genuinely useful within a protocol. Maybe, users need to stake such utility token, temporarily locking a certain amount. You can then have different tiers that get them this or that discount. Since staking prevents the short-term sale, like a form of capital control, and there is still an incentive to buy, creating buying pressure, promoters always gain.

Another perk can be governance, the beating heart of the DAO brain. An Initial Coin Offering (ICO) or a Security Token Offering (STO) are crypto alternatives to the Initial Public Offering (IPO). In a DAO, there is no management. Smart contracts will obey majorities. No "whoso pulleth out this sword of this stone and anvil, is rightwise king born of all England".

How about getting rid of paywalls? Well, this is another option, now in the context of journalism. Abbreviated news could be made available to the general public, but the most curious among them can learn more with a token of appreciation, which acts as a membership card, or a ticket, if we were talking about other services and experiences, instead of just content.

In some jurisdictions, the organisers of events, e.g. a festival, will not be legally permitted to sell alcoholic beverages. The usual workaround for its organisers is selling chips, similar to casino chips, but those can indeed be exchanged for drinks. Arguably, a digital token, purposefully launched for the event, would be more user-friendly and might provide early funding.

Spicy NFTs could be a somewhat toxic attention grabber. In line with being approached by a "hottie", whose main job is trying to sell us products or services we don't need and never will. Products or services to be then delivered by far more competent, and often less attractive, professionals, who are smart enough to know their limitations and get someone else.

As Facebook showed us, engagement is not always a positive thing, for it is often easier engaging with outrage. This is why Big Media will bombard us with sensationalist news 24/7. At this overwhelming state, caused by the barks of those herding dogs, masses are like real sheep, all predictably running in the same direction... So go create an echo chamber or do not!

Loyalty could be attained by assisting those who so desire in setting up a DIY node. Not unlike having the branch of a bank inside your habitual place of abode to serve its sole local client. This not only contributes to network decentralisation, but also, every transaction you sign is going to be posted to the blockchain through that node, without possible censors.

With all things DIY, users will immediately understand the value they are getting. They might ignore how hard it was pulling something together if it wasn't them who did it. However, if you just give them a day in your life, they will beg you to please come back. Public blockchains are all about users having the optionality and you should not prevent them from trying.

On a purely psychological level, the first provider that locks me in is the first provider I will do all in my power to get rid of. This attitude does not show confidence on their part and, if they are insecure about their own product or service, do they really expect their user base to be any less so about it? This was my reason to abandon iOS after one "spyware attempt".

Why does sincere loyalty matter? Let us say you swore allegiance to a country, the one you were born in or some other. Now you have an obligation, but you entered that covenant out of your own volition. Should you have been forced, then there would be no way to tell if you are a true believer or a traitor in the making. To choose we must have options first.

Every time you create value for your paying customers is an opportunity to get their feedback. You could do so through a system of blockchain-based reviews, e.g. if there is an action for them to sign with their wallets, they could also add a small note for your reference. That way you kill two birds with one stone, improving the product, without being secretly hated.

DAO promoters can struggle communicating with the core development team. Sometimes they will think "that is your opinion, sir". You do not want to be seen as opinionated, for they may or may not pay attention to that, especially when they can call it a day. Putting the spotlight on their work ensures they will not be "swimming naked" when the tide goes out.

Depending on how mainstream this hypothetical DAO were in its scope, you could serve only a few wealthy clients, whose situation you laser-focus on understanding, same as those profitable Swiss boutique banks, with a dozen employees. Even if the blockchain has use cases for everybody, you are just not for everybody, and neither should be your product or service.

Note that, when it comes to a new technology that is still being defined, you can figuratively kill your master, me, and be part of that redefinition, without having to wait your turn. Tomorrow you might create a concept that we, the industry dinosaurs, know nothing about and will have to learn it like everybody else. Forget respect, just try to be better than all of us.

## Global Commerce

**Lev:** In an interconnected world, small businesses are no longer confined to local markets. The rise of cryptocurrencies presents a novel approach to conducting business across borders, potentially simplifying transactions and eliminating traditional barriers. As we dive into this realm, Matías: How do cryptocurrencies facilitate global commerce for small businesses, and what are the considerations for cross-border transactions, including exchange rates and regulations?

**Matías:** Commerce has allowed us to know each other's peoples better and forge reciprocal friendships of old since the Biblical times of Tarshish, when King Solomon of Israel and Judah went into a joint venture with King Hiram of Tyre. But, while trust is being built, we need a neutral space that is not controlled by either of the parties, so exchanges will be acceptable.

Chambers of commerce are practically the only thing keeping us from following our worst instincts into the mutually assured destruction of our economies. They remind us it does not need to be that way and it is a choice. Commercial interests force leaders to keep engaging with each other, so countries decoupling to embrace protectionism is a net negative.

Not all these trade barriers are made equal though. There is, however, a technical component we cannot blame governments for, and that is the inefficiency of the financial system. You and your clients are the ones who will be footing the bill, just because a network of correspondent banks have been playing football and settling scores at one fee per intermediary.

Cryptoassets are poised to change the status quo, especially for cross-border payments pertaining to capital, goods, and services. This is not absent of challenges, like wallet-to-wallet transactions being recorded on an immutable ledger that necessitates some programmability to ensure the absence of fraud, as well as some jurisdictions specific to blockchain.

We mentioned in the past that Bitcoin had a superior settlement layer than EVM-compatible blockchains. One of the reasons is that Ethereum uses a Turing complete programming language, unlike BTC's native network, which does not. In other words, it does not have any loops or recursion, and, just like with avionics software, run times are predictable.

Bitcoin and Ethereum were conceived with different goals in mind. The former kept a simple base layer, so that settlements had little to no attack surface. The latter introduced complexities to run fancy smart contracts, which I am sure its founder regrets in retrospect, given most DApps ended up on an L2, turning Ethereums' EVM into an overly complex base layer.

That said, every public blockchain will be preferable to the house of cards where you have your deposits now. Each of those blockchains will bring their own native strengths and weaknesses to the table. Do you want it secure? Then Bitcoin or Ethereum. Do you also want it cheap/fast? Then Lightning or Polygon. You only care about privacy? Then Monero or Zcash.

Even if physical businesses get away with it, e-commerce cannot take place in a wallet-to-wallet arrangement, without the smart features of smart contracts. Imagine a customer wants to return a product or service. The platform would need to decide whether to do so in the original crypto or its fiat equivalent, perhaps introducing a FX rate risk or taxable events.

So what you do when you deploy one of these self-enforceable contracts is creating a figurative circuit that cannot be shortcut. This software knows the drill and, when a new situation is encountered, it will resolve it with the predictable outcome that was agreed upon beforehand. The absence of human error brings more trust in the system and allows it to scale well.

Many of us still remember the well-known headline of "Chicago Title gets a win in Champion-Cain's $400M Ponzi scheme case". This was a lady who basically social engineered an account manager of Chicago Title to release millions held in escrow that should have not been touched. Obviously, the title company is not the wrongdoer here, but custodianship did enable it.

From the point of view of traceability, tokenisation of real-world assets is going to transform the way commodities are bought and sold. Can you prove where your gold came from despite the best efforts of the refinery's chemists to add/remove trace impurities? With the blockchain, you can do just that. Simply list all said impurities at every step of their supply chain.

"Since the invention of the radio, the international consensus has been that the radio-waves are no one's property, and thus the interception itself is not illegal". How could this benefit trade? Pairing blockchains with servers called Software Defined Radio (SDR), land stations connected to WebSDR, OpenWebRX, or KiwiSDR that could facilitate signals intelligence.

So you do not need to be Nathan Mayer Rothschild, who is said to have sent couriers to the Battle of Waterloo, to possess early knowledge of the outcome before the British Cabinet did. An SDR system connected to Hugging Face's transformers library, specifically the opus-mt-en model, could host lightweight .txt transcripts in English on our news blockchains.

What is the revolutionary bit? With SDRs you "listen" to the entirety of the radio spectrum, even encoded channels like those used by military, police, firefighters, ambulances, and air traffic control. Big Media will not give you firsthand information of why your shipment was stopped at a checkpoint in some conflict zone, but militias have to communicate among themselves.

For the maritime industry, a public ledger that informs captains where pirates are before they are sighted can help ships change course to prevent confrontation and ultimately lose as little time as possible. Time that always costs money, but, with high inflation, even more so. This does not even take into account the impact of ransoms on insurance premiums.

We cannot talk about global commerce without mentioning commodities. As explained by Andreas Antonopoulos, who is part of the Oversight Committee for the Bitcoin Reference Rate at the Chicago Mercantile Exchange (CME), having some benchmarks to guide our futures contracts is essential, and many of those are starting to be denominated in Bitcoin.

This is huge because the CME does not target Wall Street, but producers looking to hedge their risks when selling at times of market weakness. A Brazilian farmer with soybean crops can now bypass his banking bully and run a crypto operation, with the peace of mind that, as a rural resident, he is able to use guns to protect his property and avoid a "$5 wrench attack".

In case you are not familiar with the aforementioned attack, it is basically one in which the threat of violence against you or your loved ones is used, so that you reveal your mnemonic under duress. Then, once they have your recovery phrase, they send your coins to a wallet under their control. In Brazil, some rural areas are days away from the nearest police station.

Ok, I will say it again... Freedom may not give you security, but it brings liberty! Still, for those living in places where gun laws are less loose than Brazil's, the main remedy is plausible deniability. Trezor hardware wallets will add a passphrase, which is one extra word. So that, if you do not input it, it will show another wallet with a small balance, waiting to be mugged.

Another alternative, if yours is an operation of a certain size, is creating a multisig wallet. Especially if the signatories are few and far between, then, unless a minimum threshold is threatened simultaneously, there is no way for violence to be effectively used at dispossessing you from the proceeds of your commercial interests. Do you realise how powerful this property is?

In the future, there might be even more arbitrage opportunities with a multisig. Perhaps replicating the model of the joint bank accounts, where the holder is the owner for legal and tax purposes and is domiciled in a low-tax jurisdiction, whereas the authorised user is not the owner, but he can still spend in his high-tax jurisdiction, just like if the money were his.

It could be argued that a multisig would bring more reassurances to the authorised user, for he needs to sign and the holder needs to sign too, to confirm, but, equally, he knows the holder will not squander the money before he, the authorised user, has the chance to. This can have its place for individuals and small businesses to reduce their remittance tax basis.

Non-custodial escrows like Mellifex's could be used for estate planning, based on Treas. Reg. § 1.451-2's definition of "constructive receipt of income". Suppose a taxpayer anticipates the settlement of an insurance claim, which will constitute income, unless excluded by a code provision, then, deferring a receipt to the time it offsets an expenditure, is priceless.

Global commerce requires going beyond your local mindset. You do not need to be some globalist, but it is imperative you understand what you are dealing with and have the capacity to use every trick in the book. As Terence McKenna would say, "if you don't have a plan, you become part of somebody else's plan", like the failed babysitter of somebody else's kids.

In summary, the blockchain is a Swiss army knife with tools to increase everything from trust, cybersecurity, savings, independence, resilience, traceability, reliability, hedging, freedom, decentralisation, avoidance, and planning, to many others. But it is also open for you to decide what you want it to become, so you can now be part of the driving force of change.

# Risk Management

**Lev:** The dynamic world of cryptocurrencies offers a plethora of opportunities, but not without its share of risks. For small businesses considering this path, understanding potential vulnerabilities becomes paramount. This leads us to inquire, Matías: What are the specific risks associated with accepting and holding cryptocurrencies for a small business, and how can these risks be mitigated through proper management and insurance?

**Matías:** The primary risk is the fact that your wallet is open to receive airdrops from any other within its blockchain, even if/when this was an unsolicited payment. Therefore, when OFAC sanctioned the Tornado Cash smart contract, which tainted any wallet address that interacted with it, pranksters used such an opportunity to get celebrity wallets also tainted.

Of course, centralised issuers like Circle prevented their USDC token from entering or exiting these tainted wallets to avoid contagion. This is one way to go, but, as my great grandmother used to say, "the more you can do, the more you will be asked to do". She did not think of regulators, but it ended up being this way, for decentralisation will spread responsibilities.

Even with the Travel Rule for cryptoasset service providers, desperately trying to make the idea of a Decentralised Autonomous Organisation (DAO) a thing of the past, by also requiring those to store any Personal Identifier Information (PII), DAOs are springing up like mushrooms. After all, what if the founders are already dead with no one in charge anymore?

This is not a radical thought. Remember, Bitcoin was not cracked down on, primarily because Satoshi was never identified and, by the time the authorities woke up to the fact that Bitcoin could one day challenge fiat, it was too late or too costly for them to attack the network. Other protocols are using Bitcoin's experience as a blueprint for their own P2P solutions.

So, while providers are having an increasingly hard time structuring themselves the right way to keep their crypto offerings competitive against traditional banking, generally speaking, if you find a non-KYCed exchange, however they did it, it is not illegal for you to use. My guess is that alternative distribution channels for crypto software will be created.

If you visited Cuba in the 2000s, you would know there were no streaming services on their heavily censored internet. Nonetheless, cunning Cubans always managed to get their hands on movie files, which they shared physically through a rudimentary system of USB flash drive couriers. This move avoided a more North Korea-style isolation from the outside world.

One possible way our industry might evolve, if its regulations become unbearable in terms of privacy or lack thereof, is removing the platform. How? By distributing the tools as client-side programs that connect to no server other than a blockchain network, directly from the user's own desktop, treating it as a node. Users could choose self-reporting... Or not!

"Global compliance costs of the order of $304 billion [...] manage to seize around $3 billion a year". Think about it for a second, $301 billion of shareholder value are being destroyed. One does not even need to be a Politically Exposed Person (PEP) anymore, as many of those banks do not reveal the reason why the accounts were closed, so it is what suits them.

They will not admit they closed an account on the grounds of age, caste, disability, language, name, nationality, race/ethnicity, region, religion, or sex/gender, among others, but the reality of it is, unless laws change, they can do it. I am waiting for a brave lawmaker who says "we tried KYC-AML, it did not work, so our jurisdiction will now get rid of this once and for all".

This is not much of a risk for large economies and I could actually see the UK, under certain conditions, getting rid of KYC-AML, if Brexiteers have it their way. To seal the deal, HMRC should also allow its taxes to be paid in crypto. The only thing preventing crypto-only businesses is that, in most countries, but not all, taxes are denominated and paid in the legal tender.

Taxes denominated in the crypto in which earnings were received might seem like a small detail, but it is not. This proposal would help stabilise crypto-only businesses, no longer having to arbitrarily measure their performance in another currency. Why should they if they are ok with the idea of accepting, say, Bitcoin and their business partners accept it too?

You might have heard this already, but, generally speaking, cryptoassets are far from being the ideal vehicle to launder money. In most cases, all it will take is a forensic analyst, e.g. Chainalysis, basically following the money on-chain, as opposed to digging into records of less transparent financial service providers, hiding dirty laundry. Want to see an example?

If Ukrainian oligarch Serhiy Kurchenko was sanctioned by the EU and the US, HSBC would simply call him Adrian Matthew Bradley, their "bonafide" Belizean client, who doe not exist, so such name would not be part of any sanctions lists and would trigger no red flags. This is not a hypothetical; the International Consortium of Investigative Journalists (ICIJ) confirmed it.

Surprised? Well, just take a look at the amount of decoy names that are registered as UBOs of UK entities on its Companies House. Let us see, we have a "Holy Jesus Christ", whose occupation is listed as "Creator", with "Angelic" nationality and country of residence being "Heaven". It will not be the first time some Jew says this, but... This Jesus guy looks like a fake!

Jokes aside, as I mentioned in the past, there is indeed fraud going on, but, if the war on drugs has taught us anything, is that neglecting the demand side entirely, causes like the lack of financial education in this case, while solely targeting the supply side, increases profitability for criminals, who will take the risk. Plus, education is cheaper than policing.

Perhaps it is a matter of perverse incentives. In some places, institutions see themselves as service providers, while in others, they regard you as their product. In Switzerland, tax evasion, where taxpayers fail to declare income and/or assets, is a fineable offence, not a crime. In Spain, the tax authorities will geolocate smartphones in search of undeclared residents.

As a businessman I know would say, "paying an exit tax, however punitive it might be, and never coming back, is probably worth it". After all, he retained the most vital part of his net worth, his network, enabling him to connect the old country with the new one. Essentially, he became a "trade ambassador", achieving the positive ROI a few months after his departure.

If you are in crypto, you should build a passport portfolio for: 1) freedom of movement, even in houseboats or motorhomes, 2) travelling with a non-aligned document to avoid becoming some bargaining chip in a terrorist ransom, 3) securing dirt-cheap deals with limited foreign ownership, or 4) asset protection, if your country of origin is not as trustworthy anymore.

Nomadic peoples have always managed to preserve multi-generational riches, despite being prevented from owning land by the ruler of the day, and there are valuable lessons to be learnt there. Imagine what those individuals could have achieved with "brain wallets" and the ability to store BTC in their minds by memorising the mnemonic recovery phrases.

The reason seeds refuse to grow in deserts is not a lack of moisture, but the fact that the soil keeps moving underneath, resulting in uncertainty and causing that "investment" to go elsewhere where it is more likely to thrive. Therefore, if politics is a game of chess, we might wish our camp checkmates, but we will need to force a stalemate for the common good.

Why am I discussing this? Well, because crypto markets are volatile in nature and, if a business waits until the last minute to relocate, not only could its tax bill be impacted, but new crypto laws might pass that complicate matters in unforeseeable ways. You want to be proactive, not reactive, even if it was not your ideal timing, but the last chance you have.

Another "risk", if we can call it as such, is that, due to the low barriers to entry, this is not an industry where you can "set it and forget it". Its underlying technology evolves at the speed of the internet, and what is possible today pales in comparison to what will be achievable in, say, a few years' time. You cannot rest on the laurels of your earliest successes.

In any case, this competition decreases the threat posed by outdated systems that have not been patched for years. Seen in a certain light, every DApp is an open bounty for hackers to try to claim for themselves. Initially, the jackpot is small and it grows over time, so a DApp like MakerDAO, that has been around for a long time, has proven its resilience.

The blockchain purges itself! We know there will never be more than 21 million Bitcoin, but this is not the real number in circulation. What I mean is that, over the years, there have been countless wallet owners who, not fully appreciating the value of their holdings, mismanaged their seeds and got themselves locked out, thereby increasing the value of accessible BTC.

Your loss will decrease the coin's effective supply and will be someone else's gain, by virtue of limiting potential selling pressures. This does not need to happen to your business, so doing things the right way, where others do not, earns you bonus points. We can refer to this as our "dumb tax", a deflation mechanism that will reward the smartest of all HODLers.

## Taxation and Accounting

**Lev:** The introduction of cryptocurrencies into mainstream business operations has inevitably led to questions about their implications for financial reporting and regulatory compliance. As authorities grapple with these new-age assets, businesses must stay abreast of the changing landscape. Thus, the pressing question becomes, Matías: How do cryptocurrencies impact the taxation and accounting practices of a small business, and what resources are available to ensure compliance with local laws?

**Matías:** Beyond the admittedly snobbish fact that Velociraptor is Latin for "swift thief" and some will argue this would make an excellent moniker for most Western tax authorities. There are several parallels between taxes and dinosaurs, more nuanced perhaps and, I hope, offering you a read that is educational, entertaining, and generous in terms of dry-wit humour.

According to the Australian Museum, "some theropods like Albertosaurus and Giganotosaurus possibly attacked with a 'bite and slice' technique rather than going for an outright kill". This approach allowed them to prey on large sauropods, letting those heal enough to survive for a while. In essence, a sustainable feeding behaviour that did not need of any freezer.

Western democracies are becoming increasingly demagogic, even if we rationally understand that rhetoric is to politics what pastry baking is to medicine, and cosmetics to gymnastics. They operate with total disregard for sustainability, driven by the incentive for governments to opt for an "outright kill" and feast now, leaving the caloric deficit for the next in line.

Cryptoassets are a blessing for financial hubs bullied by the OECD, the lobby for high-tax countries. Until recently, the stigma of the "tax haven" label was almost a death sentence, not for reputational reasons, but for practical ones. You needed a US correspondent bank for your offshore entity to move dollars in and out. But what if you leave this dollar system?

Started by London lawyers at the time of the British Empire, many these hubs knew that competing with continental nations, with enough population to sustain industry, was not viable. The only resource they could export was their laws, so legal fiction became their best-selling "literary genre" until the PATRIOT Act. Crypto ended this existential crisis.

When Salvadoran president Nayib Bukele took the unprecedented step of adopting Bitcoin as legal tender, El Salvador became the largest country to do so. Despite critics wishing him to fail, he did not, effectively ending decades of US "exorbitant power" in the region. This move did not go unnoticed, sparking a dedollarisation trend across the entire Global South.

As it has emerged, third-world countries have been net creditors to the developed world, rather than debtors. They reaped none of the benefits, for having been forcibly integrated into a system that was rigged against them. Now they are offering aggressive tax exemptions to siphon off the liquidity from Western crypto markets, satisfying an unquenchable thirst.

This scenario echoes a time in history when, following their expulsion from Iberia, many Sephardic Jews hurried to secure their letters of marque and reprisal. This initiated a golden age of legalised piracy against the gold fleet of an empire that had seized their homes, homes that their keys would not open anymore: an onerous debt worth repaying with interests.

In due course, this tax competition, which now lacks a central kill switch, will compel the West to adopt more frugal policies if they wish to retain the cash cows within their tax net. This phenomenon is already manifest within the EU, where our Freedom of Establishment is penalising all member states that failed to implement the necessary austerity measures.

Slavoj Žižek tacitly admits that the international left is clueless about what to do the day after their revolution, once they have seized power. "Red aristocrats" could not care less for their subjects, but find themselves at a crossroads, not to be perceived as the "enemy of the people". Our industry is despised in the EU corridors of power, unless enriching third countries.

Wasteful politicians think "if only I had more to work with", ignoring what satisfied ladies say, "it depends how you use it". While there are still a few loopholes in the Old Continent pertaining to crypto, they might be sealed by the time you read this, owing to the efforts of tax harmonisation within the union. So please bear in mind taxation will always be a moving target.

In Germany, Malta, Portugal, and Switzerland, there is neither VAT nor long-term capital gains tax on Bitcoin. In Belarus, crypto taxes have been suspended until 2025. In Georgia, any tax implications will hinge on territoriality. Hence, no capital gains, short- or long-term, nor income tax on Bitcoin, provided it was not Georgian. This will apply to fiat income too.

El Salvador exempts foreigners from crypto taxes, and BTC must be accepted by all merchants. Singapore and Malaysia offer full exemptions on your coin's gains and partially exempt income to varying degrees. In Puerto Rico, there are no BTC capital gains but a reduced rate of territorial income tax. As for Bermuda, the Cayman Islands, and the UAE... Nothing!

Clearly, countries that are generally tax-free will be so for crypto too, making the list longer. However, there are benefits to opting for "onshore" countries that are not universally tax-free. By not being regarded as tax havens, these tend to fly under the radar, resulting in a lower cost of living. If your income and assets are exempt, do everyone else's matter?

It is important to note that tax is just one of many costs for individuals and small businesses alike, e.g. Monaco may not be the best location for wealth creation. When larger economies, home to big and small fish, extend temporary incentives, it would be prudent to seize them. After all, tax exemptions are a reward for doing all your jurisdiction wanted you to.

Contrary to popular belief, I am not opposed to the moderate use of free market tools in a carrot and stick approach. You do not want cars in London and wish to impose a congestion charge? Fine, but in turn, you also offer a near full exemption for those creating new woodland sites, as is the case, encouraging them to take a multi-year risk for those rewards.

In addition to the taxes themselves, be aware that not all accountants pick up the gauntlet. Some jurisdictions, like the Netherlands, complicate matters further. Here, cryptoassets are not taxed as gains but based on the net worth of the assets on January 1st. This applies to natural persons and some juridical entities not already subject to a government tax ruling.

At times, legislative errors and omissions are narrowly avoided. This might have been the case in the UK when its Treasury Committee nearly equated consumer trading of unbacked crypto to gambling. A bizarre notion, but had it been adopted, those profits would have been tax-free, just like gambling's: not what Tories, now governing like Labour, desired.

Fortunately, bookkeeping has a fool-proof aspect. Should you forget to record a crypto transaction, you can always refer back to the public ledger on the blockchain. However, it is worth noting that tax authorities have the same ability to access this information. Therefore, any mistake your accountant makes will be obvious to a casual observer, raising the stakes.

Sometimes, small businesses, and the individuals behind them, come to the conclusion that it is better not to be under that sword of Damocles. There are countries that will simply cause fewer headaches overall and might even offer better weather than their current locations. As you grow older, you will find that you lack the time and energy for all this nonsense.

The reality in much of the West is that a crypto business, or any business for that matter, will spend too much time focusing on laws and taxes, and not enough doing what they do best. This creates drag and slows the pace at which a business can grow. Intuitively, the same business in some tax haven, will do twice as good, while losing less than half its annual capital.

It is important to remember that a company has the mandate to maximise shareholder value, meaning its management cannot take actions such as arbitrarily forgiving a borrower's debt. Some left-leaning acquaintances believe this the case. But if they were company executives, they would not go to jail over it after shareholders sue them for breach of fiduciary duty.

We all have our preferences, but once you are part of management, you must do what is best for your company's future and that of its owners. Sometimes this involves moving operations, other times it means being acquired by a larger entity through M&A. Such is life, and you need to accept it, even if/when it results in an exit that will conclude your services.

The jurisdiction will always dictate the tax rate, but you are the one who chooses the jurisdiction. So ultimately, users hold the power to terminate their usage, and over time, the free market will penalise those offering little value for money. A decline in actual taxpayers is the only way to instigate change. Ireland had to endure hardship to foster new growth.

Is there anyone in 2023 who doubts that Leprechaun economics works? The government even had to alter the method of calculating Irish GDP because a country growing at an annual rate exceeding 26% did not make sense. Now, with Brexit and Switzerland tacitly taking sides in Ukraine, business-friendly and neutral Ireland is experiencing a second resurgence.

As Oscar Wilde would say, "the only way to get rid of a temptation is to yield to it". If a country is heading in the wrong direction, do not fight it, remove yourself from the equation. Guided by Karl Marx, they may end up bankrupt, but the good news is that another David Hasselhoff will tear down that metaphorical Berlin Wall. You can profit from the recovery then.

## Innovation and Growth

**Lev:** In the pursuit of growth and innovation, small businesses frequently turn to emerging technologies to gain a competitive edge. Cryptocurrencies, more than just a transaction medium, can potentially act as a catalyst for business transformation. Matías, how can cryptocurrencies spur innovation and growth within a small business, and what are the potential challenges and opportunities that come with adopting this technology?

**Matías:** Machiavelli noted that one must possess the cunning of a fox to recognise traps and the strength of a lion to frighten the wolves, but it demands a particularly diagonal thinker to achieve both. CEOs struggle with this corporate balance: being startups, moving faster than regulation, or established companies, trying to slow all others around with regulation.

The concoctions of pseudo-innovators arise from selectively picking the buzzwords of the day and throwing them into a blender, hoping for a coherent concept to emerge with minimal mental exertion. Such "innovations" are typically birthed by institutions that can shoulder the sunk costs of a publicity stunt. Welcome to Jersey's brand-new data trusts.

In theory, a system like this could function utilising the previously discussed Zero Knowledge Proofs (ZKP), wherein the verifier, e.g. the trustee, ascertains the truthfulness the truthfulness of the information without knowing it. A far cry from their proposed custody, where merely peeping at the data, even without taking possession, would be too much.

Are the Crown Dependencies not part of the Five Eyes (FVEY) alliance? Then I would not blindly trust data protection without a stabilisation, or freezing clause, that would render any discovery stemming from such trust as inadmissible evidence in a court of law. Perhaps preemptively sharing a few different falsehoods with trustees to identify the informant.

Abraham Maslow stated, "I suppose it is tempting, if the only tool you have is a hammer, to treat everything as if it were a nail". While this book elucidates many of the technological possibilities of blockchain, I do not want you to become that hammerer. Any correct approach involves identifying the problem first, not finding a problem to suit your solutions.

Innovation frequently encompasses two facets: divergent thinking, where dreamers like myself expend all their free time, and convergent thinking, where we return to reality after being reminded by the more the "adults in the room" that a concrete execution of our ideas is expected. The former is essential for true originality, while the latter ensures its practical utility.

While everyone has a different approach and teaching innovation is not an exact science, I have noticed several commonalities in the moments that spark it for me and other innovators. Firstly, an experience is necessary, something previously unseen. This trigger a slight chaos in your mind, then, a period of isolation, will allow for the necessary space to process it.

Speaking of innovative developments, once you launch your protocol, brace yourself for a gradual loss of control over it, a control that will be increasingly assumed by your own community. Smart contracts will not change after being deployed. What is more likely is the occurrence of some hard fork, akin to what divided Bitcoin (BTC) and Bitcoin Cash (BCH).

Personally, I believe the primary value of open source lies in its unique distribution. It hinders censorship attempts, e.g. perhaps you published a book containing a few lines of code that readers can copy and paste, resulting in this codebase being hosted on thousands of repositories. The beauty of it? You can still earn your living handsomely while others use it.

Moreover, it affords plausible deniability, as, once derivative work, your code "for educational purposes only", absolves you of any compliance responsibilities. If users bypass KYC-AML procedures, that is a matter of concern for the relevant parties, not you. For those of you who prioritise privacy, the approach offers a golden opportunity to legitimately attain it.

Our authorities no longer regulate the technology akin to pharmaceuticals, they expect providers to police users. However, remember that code cannot be censored. This is the format to distribute your tools. Of course, you can strive to make them somewhat user-friendly, but do not become the weak link in your chain. Like Satoshi... You must spear and disappear!

A revolutionary solution will earn you many powerless friends and a few powerful enemies. You need to be prepared to not only launch without revealing your identity but also to navigate the tax laws when justifying the origins of your monies: countries like Israel offer their new immigrants a generous decade-long exemption from reporting income and/or assets.

These challenges will introduce a thrilling element into your life, as you harbour a secret that is yours alone, adding to its specialness. However, you must concoct a believable cover for what you do for a living, given that it is a common conversational icebreaker, and you want to be entirely convincing. Opt for nothing flamboyant, but a dull job, hard to remember.

You might perceive this as an exaggeration, yet unless you aspire to be a CEX that maintains a friendly rapport with the government while being hostile to the very citizens that government represents, you will have to make sacrifices. It will not be easy and it might not suit you. However, if you are inclined towards this path, all subsequent choices will align with it.

I was taken aback by Brian Armstrong's statements. Here is a man who founded the largest centralised exchange in America, doing everything in his power to please regulators. His dismay was evident, not solely because Coinbase faced a lawsuit from the SEC, but due to the realisation that his company had relinquished numerous cool innovations, holding them back:

> **"Flatcoin"** aims to create a "superior" cryptocurrency to Bitcoin by being fully decentralized and tracking consumer prices to maintain purchasing power. This could involve asset backing or algorithms to avoid inflation and seizure risks seen in some more popular fiat-backed stablecoins. It draws inspiration from projects like Ampleforth/Spot, Nuon, and Truflation.

> **"Onchain reputation"** proposes some decentralised protocol to assign reputation scores to addresses or ENS names, based on onchain data, similar to PageRank for websites. This could be used for decentralised lending, merchant ratings, fraud prevention, airdrops, etc. It emphasises the need for decentralisation to prevent any form of capture or abuse.

**"Onchain ads"** wants to go beyond traditional ads by paying for user actions (CPA). Smart contracts can offer rewards for referrals, creating ad inventory. Wallets and DApps can route users to these contracts and earn when users engage in this multi-level marketing of sorts. Real-time auctions may optimise pricing. Examples include Spindl and HypeLab.

**"Onchain capital formation"** envisions a version of ICOs for easier global capital raising. It combines features of Stripe Atlas and AngelList, helping Web3 entrepreneurs register ventures pseudonymously and raise funds transparently, through pitch decks, discussions, and ratings. Democratised fundraising could, therefore, unleash entrepreneurial potential worldwide.

**"Job/task marketplace for crypto"** seeks to overcome any cross-border payment barriers by enabling jobs and tasks that pay in cryptocurrency. I assume, a non-custodial escrow would be deeply needed for a use case like the one proposed. This concept promotes a more accessible and borderless job market, similar to platforms like Braintrust and Earn.com.

**"Privacy for layer 2"**, bringing privacy to L2 crypto solutions is a growing concern due to the public nature of most transactions. Exploring privacy solutions like Aztec, Polygon, and zkSync presents a potential business opportunity in enhancing it to meet demant. These three examples rely on the Zero Knowledge Proofs (ZKP) our friend Avi Wigderson helped explain.

**"P2P exchange fully onchain"**, creating a fully decentralized P2P exchange onchain is essential for preserving our personal freedoms and avoiding centralised shutdown pressures, as Armstrong himself knows all too well. Such an exchange could incorporate escrow, reputation, and mediation, as exemplified by projects, partially achieving some of those, like Onboard.

**"Onchain games"**, the intersection of crypto and games is still evolving. Exploring ownership of in-game items through NFTs as already mentioned, and building persistent virtual worlds, inspired by projects like Dark Forest and Loot, presents exciting opportunities. Other examples include Azra Games, Horizon Blockchain Games, Immutable, Plai Labs, and Yuga Labs.

**"Tokenising real world assets"**, tokenising any real-world assets, like USDC, on blockchain networks, opens the door to more programmable, composable, and globally liquid financial primitives. Numerous projects, including Goldfinch, Centrifuge, MoHash, Naos, and Mountain Protocol, explore tokenisation of various assets, from debt instruments to luxury.

**"Software to start and manage network states"**, Balaji Srinivasan's concept of the "Network State" sparked interest in startup cities and similar initiatives. There is a growing need for software to facilitate governance, voting, fundraising, citizenship, taxation, and services within these states, potentially benefiting various types of such communities.

**"Web3 professional network"**, aka Web3 LinkedIn, envisions professional networks using non-transferable NFTs to verify employment, education, and other credentials. Users own and monetise their network, fostering transparency and confidence in skills. Open standards enable onchain resumes and more clear criteria for both, employers and collaborators.

## Sustainability and Ethics

**Lev:** The ethos of a business is often reflected in its practices and choices. As cryptocurrencies gain traction, their alignment with sustainability and ethical considerations becomes a focal point for discerning businesses. Matías, in this realm, how can a small business align its use of cryptocurrencies with its sustainability and ethical goals, and what are the potential conflicts or synergies in this area?

**Matías:** Let us start by establishing what ethics is, because it cannot be separated from the idea of justice, which is about knowing when to be indulgent or "good" and when to be ruthless or "bad". This is not about the sentimental stories that once captivated the Judeo-Christian world, about gentleman known for turning the other cheek... Social justice is not just!

Social justice warriors often disregard reality, that little thing based on objective facts, focusing solely on how individuals feel about it. A mindset of "I am offended, therefore you must have said something offensive to me". This is a slippery slope for science, where scientists are supposed to be brave enough to challenge each other using the scientific method only.

But masses gravitate towards simplistic answers, like Assembly Bill (AB) 979 and Senate Bill (SB) 826, which required public companies in California to diversify boards with a specific number of "underrepresented" directors and maintain statutory gender diversity. This violated the Equal Protection Clause of the 14th Amendment according to the Superior Court.

This obsession with equity could have led to a situation where, if you identified as a Pacific Islander, 0.5% population, you could free up your schedule to attend board meetings for the rest of your life. Nobody would ask for your experience in whatever the company does. Democrats did assume that some individuals would never succeed based on meritocracy.

As the clinical psychologist Simon Baron-Cohen elucidated through his Empathising-Systemising (E-S) theory, on autism and the neurological differences between females and males: the former tend to interested in people and the latter in things. In a scenario where gents were fewer, would it be fair to hire the best females available and all male applicants?

When phrased that way, it does not seem to hold much logic, does it? However, it is crucial to understand that smart contracts are neither good nor bad, they simply operate as they were pre-programmed to. In this context, an AI hybrid could potentially embody the personality traits that shareholders desire in their company's managers. So how to achieve this?

Blockchain technologies could help the "transhuman" version of successful management teams run a company, even from the grave. I am sure the irreplaceable Larry Ellison has already thought about it as part of Oracle's business continuity planning. So smart contract could allocate capital as this team would and shareholders can update the algorithm if it fails them.

Now, imagine AI model dubbed "Oracle management 2023" or "SpaceX management 2023". Even in the absence of the original team members, thousands small businesses could, instead of hiring McKinsey & Company for overpriced advice, leverage Elon Musk to elevate their operations to unprecedented heights, while paying Musk's heirs a royalty for his mind.

If the market has trusted your leadership for decades, that criteria for making decisions can be used to train a self-enforceable AI-based contract. In a way, your synthetic consciousness would thus be able to interact with the world of the living and grow the company for millennia, well into the space age. But who is accountable for "hardcoded ethics"?

Perhaps you are not familiar with ethical wills, e.g. tzava'ot, like the one a Brazilian cousin recently showed me. The primary objective of these is to pass ethical values from one generation to the next. Family businesses know ethical "trade secrets" are a source of success, but a transhuman version of the late patriarch could serve as a liability discharge for heirs.

Not unlike the Schrödinger's cat situation in which Lee Kun-hee, son of Samsung's founder, was hospitalised in 2014 and declared legally dead in 2020, despite rumors his heirs were only delaying what would be the largest inheritance tax bill in history, 12 trillion won or 10.78 billion dollars, with strategic ambiguity... If true, I may have to take my hat off to them!

Unless governance is truly transparent, you would not invest in businesses whose management can withhold relevant details or manufacture crises just to manipulate you, akin to Joseph Goebbels with his philosophy of "all you have to do is tell them they are being attacked and denounce the pacifists for lack of patriotism and exposing the country to danger". Right?

So there you have it! What will differentiate your sustainability and ethics from those who fake it, is that if you opt for the right blockchain solution, is that yours is genuinely true. Not merely because you assert it, but because anyone can verify it without having to trust any of your prior claims. Higher management cannot take the company hostage anymore.

This is, of course, a must, since, as we have already discussed, ESG rating entities can, and often do, give subjective scores. But this should not surprise you. It is the same with other institutions like VC firms: a startup raises capital initially for being good friends with a General Partner (GP) and only subsequently for being deemed, well, a semi-decent investment.

Oh! Sorry, I should not have said that... Of course, we live in a perfectly fair world with unicorns and rainbows, especially in Silicon Valley. Although to be precise, there are more rainbows and fewer unicorns by the day. Still, you should deal with what you can measure beyond PR. What are the most common values? This will avoid you pitching to the wrong crowds.

However, such is not the approach of most businesses. They will embrace ideas that are perceived as fashionable, but, statistically speaking, those are elitist and, quite possibly, do not even resonate with your average client. The role of a company is not to patronise anybody. Users do not need to adapt and can go use the next provider that wants their business.

As Jeremy's Razors would say in a genius commercial, "stop giving your money to woke corporations that hate you", and I would add, "give it to a DAO, unless you hate yourself". That said, if your values are genuine, it is a matter of time until even your worst critics will sort their differences with your brand and respect what it stands for, which gently enlightened them.

The best person to illustrate this is a dear friend from my community, who is a world-class heart surgeon. Yes, he would still save a dying man who has a swastika tattoo, no matter how much animosity he felt deep inside. After all, we are defined by how we treat our enemies. We can totally wage our "unholy" wars in self-defence, but not by becoming "inhumane".

Consensus algorithms like those of blockchains are a metaphor for the way we resolve conflicts with ourselves and others. Most of us had never experienced a lockdown before COVID-19 and, without necessarily being anti-vax, we understood what was coming, along with constitutional dictatorship. We knew it would leave a scar that would not heal for years.

Luke Kemp, a researcher at the Centre for the Study of Existential Risk (CSER) at the Cambridge, said it best: "during an emergency, the knee-jerk reaction is always to stomp down, to reinforce those atop hierarchies in the state and significantly curtail the freedoms, voice, and agency of citizens, often in a draconian fashion. I call this the 'Stomp Reflex'". Amen!

Central planners keep looking for answers as to what is wrong, and I would invite them to visit an animal shelter. Perhaps then they would see the correlation: dog inside a cage is upset, and dog outside a cage is happy. Unfortunately, I guess they are busy destroying incriminating evidence, in case the Nuremberg principles become fully applicable to them one day.

But representative democracy is fundamentally a scam. You think you are deciding, when this is merely a referendum on the actual decision-maker, who has already been pre-vetted by the unelected officials who put him where he is, by funding his campaign. I have read studies that proved popular sortition would actually lead to more representative governments.

Athens referred to this as isonomia, Venice as brevia, and even Friedrich Hayek proposed giving "demarchy" a chance. The idea is the same: our representatives would be selected by lottery, and any citizen of age has an equal chance to become one. This prevents special interest groups from rigging the system... Who to tap in this 100% unpredictable scenario?

Up until very recently, we did not have the means to ensure that millions of eligible citizens would be included in something like a public ledger, with an open algorithm, so that we could verify the process was random, but now we do. Another advantage is that this would negate the possibility of foreign electoral intervention, as anybody could become president here.

Cryptoassets can be adopted for ethical, pragmatic, or political reasons, but there is no such thing as a user who did not find those assets while running away from something else. They will be there for you when you need them most, and they will serve people from all walks of life, without asking who they were. A jurisdiction akin to the Biblical cities of refuge.

I am advocating for financial services to become another human right. The domain of money must free itself from any governmental codependency, with an internationally recognised professional privilege for providers to protect the interests of their clients, making those finances confidential. Only then will banking be unchained... Fulfilling our prophetic book title!

## FINAL WORD

As we stand on the cusp of a financial revolution, it is only fitting that we turn to the words of those who have been pioneers, visionaries, and critics in the world of cryptocurrencies. Their insights, drawn from various walks of life, echo the transformative potential that cryptoassets hold for humanity.

Bill Gates once remarked, "Bitcoin is exciting because it shows how cheap it can be. Bitcoin is better than currency in that you don't have to be physically in the same place and, of course, for large transactions, currency can get pretty inconvenient".

Echoing this sentiment, Richard Branson noted, "Well, I think it is working. There may be other currencies like it that may be even better. But in the meantime, there's a big industry around Bitcoin".

The world of cryptoassets is not without its critics. Warren Buffet has been vocal about his skepticism, stating, "Stay away from it. It's a mirage, basically". Yet, even amidst criticism, the crypto space has burgeoned, showcasing resilience and an innate capacity to evolve.

Elon Musk, a man synonymous with innovation and forward-thinking, has been a proponent of cryptocurrencies, emphasizing their role in facilitating financial freedom. His endorsement of Dogecoin stands as a testament to the playful yet potent potential of cryptoassets.

As we forge ahead into this uncharted territory, it is essential to approach with a discerning eye, recognizing both the opportunities and the risks involved. Christine Lagarde, the President of the European Central Bank, advises, "We should be happier to have a job than to have our savings protected. I think that it is in this spirit that monetary policy has been decided by my predecessors and I think they made quite a favorable judgment".

In conclusion, the realm of cryptoassets stands before us, offering the potential for a more inclusive, decentralized, and efficient financial ecosystem. This emerging landscape promises a redistribution of financial governance, paving the way for unprecedented innovation and growth. Yet, it is essential to acknowledge that this system is not without its flaws; it is far from perfect. It harbors vulnerabilities that necessitate comprehensive legislative measures to ensure safety and prevent misuse. Despite these challenges, for those eager to carve out a fresh path in their financial journey, this field undeniably holds a wealth of opportunities ripe for exploration and cultivation.

As Nassim Nicholas Taleb, a scholar and risk analyst, succinctly puts it, "Bitcoin's mere existence is an insurance policy that will remind governments that the last object establishment could control, namely, the currency, is no longer their monopoly. This gives us, the crowd, an insurance policy against an Orwellian future".

Finally, In the dynamic landscape of financial evolution, "Banking Unchained: How Cryptocurrencies Can Transform Your Financial Life" has guided you through the intricate pathways of the crypto revolution, a journey from the rudimentary understanding of cryptocurrencies to the sophisticated realms of onchain operations and the boundless opportunities they herald.

As we stand on the cusp of a new era, it is imperative to grasp that cryptocurrencies are not just a financial instrument; they are a transformative force, a beacon of freedom offering autonomy and empowerment in a world that is increasingly digital. This book has elucidated the mechanisms through which cryptocurrencies can foster innovation, drive growth, and facilitate a more inclusive and democratic financial ecosystem.

We delved deep into the nuances of tax regulations across different jurisdictions, offering a roadmap to navigate the complex terrains of crypto taxation and the potential havens that promise a more conducive environment for crypto enthusiasts and entrepreneurs alike. The discourse on the regulatory dynamics underscored the importance of being well-informed and adaptable, ready to seize the opportunities that lie in the ever-evolving crypto space.

The exploration of innovative concepts such as "Flatcoin", "Onchain reputation", and "Onchain capital formation" opened up vistas of opportunities waiting to be seized. These nascent ideas beckon the pioneers of tomorrow to build upon them, to forge paths untrodden, and to create solutions that are as revolutionary as they are necessary in the contemporary world.

As we navigated the intricate world of onchain operations, from ads to games, the book illuminated the potential of blockchain technology to redefine industries and create ecosystems that are transparent, decentralized, and user-empowered. The discussion on tokenising real-world assets and the envisioning of Web3 professional networks painted a picture of a future where technology and innovation walk hand in hand, creating a world of limitless possibilities.

But beyond the technicalities and the innovations, "Banking Unchained" has been a clarion call to the individual — to you. It is a call to action, urging you to step into the frontier of financial revolution with knowledge, foresight, and the courage to innovate. It is a call to embrace the future with open arms, to be the creator of opportunities, and to be the master of your financial destiny.

As we close this chapter, let us carry forward the spirit of innovation, the courage to dream, and the determination to create. Let us be the architects of a future that is decentralized, democratic, and truly ours. Let us forge ahead with the knowledge garnered and the insights gained, ready to carve out paths of financial freedom and empowerment.

Remember, the future is not something that happens to us; it is something we create. As you stand at the precipice of this brave new world, armed with the knowledge and insights from "Banking Unchained", remember that you are not just a participant in this revolution; you are a catalyst, a force of change, ready to unchain the boundless potential that lies within you and the world of cryptocurrencies.

So, as you turn this final page, step forth with determination and vision. The world of "Banking Unchained" is not just a concept; it is a reality waiting to be shaped, a canvas waiting to be painted by visionaries like you. Let us embark on this journey of creation, for the future is bright, the future is crypto, and the future is yours to shape. Let's build it, unchained and unlimited.

We hope that this reading has been both meaningful and valuable for you.

**Lev & Matías**

# GLOSSARY

**Backdoor:** A covert or unauthorised access pathway in hardware or software that circumvents typical security controls. It allows privileged users to gain entry, potentially compromising system integrity, privacy, or security. Backdoors can be created maliciously, intentionally by vendors, or due to security vulnerabilities, posing a significant cybersecurity risk.

**CBDC:** A Central Bank Digital Currency is a digital form of a nation's official currency issued and regulated by the central bank. While advertising financial inclusion benefits, there are serious concerns about its dangers, such as Orwellian surveillance. CBDCs could indeed enable governments to monitor and take over the finances of citizens unilaterally.

**Chaumian CoinJoin:** Invented by David Chaum, this is a privacy technique for cryptocurrencies. It blends multiple users' transactions into one, obscuring sources and destinations. By mixing inputs and outputs, it randomises transaction origins, enhancing the anonymity set and making it difficult to trace specific transactions on the blockchain. His CoinJoin is still considered the best.

**Cryptoassets:** The most common being cryptocurrencies, are digital or virtual assets built on blockchain technology. They might serve as a medium of exchange, store of value, or simply have a particular utility within decentralised networks. Examples of currencies include Bitcoin and Ethereum, with features like decentralisation, security, and transparency.

**DAO:** Decentralised Autonomous Organisations are smart contract-driven entities on a blockchain, governed by code and its participants. The DAO, an early example, was an investor-directed venture capital fund on Ethereum. It allowed token holders to make decisions collectively, but early vulnerabilities led to a contentious hard fork and its eventual demise.

**Dedollarisation:** The strategic reduction of reliance on the US dollar in international trade and finance. BRICS (Brazil, Russia, India, China, South Africa) and other countries are seeking a multipolar world to reduce the dominance of the USD, promoting their own currencies and fostering a more balanced global financial system to enhance economic sovereignty.

**DCA:** Dollar-Cost Averaging is an investment strategy where you regularly invest a fixed amount of money into an asset, such as stocks or cryptocurrencies, regardless of market price fluctuations. This approach reduces the impact of market volatility, potentially lowering the average purchase price over time and spreading risk for most long-term investors.

**DLC:** Discreet Log Contracts are smart contracts on the Bitcoin Network that allow for off-chain data to trigger and settle on-chain agreements. They offer privacy and scalability advantages by not revealing contract details on the blockchain until settlement, making them suitable for various applications, from decentralised finance to prediction markets and others.

**dVPN:** A decentralised Virtual Private Network is a P2P network that enables users to establish secure, private connections through distributed infrastructure, often utilising blockchain technology for authentication and routing. It enhances online privacy and security by masking IP addresses and encrypting data, promoting censorship resistance and user control.

**ENS:** Ethereum Name Service is a decentralised domain name system built on the Ethereum blockchain for a new uncensorable internet. It assigns human-readable domains to complex Ethereum addresses. This ENS enables decentralised web hosting, where the file location is determined by its unique identifier or hash, not by any specific server or location.

**Escrow:** A financial arrangement where assets or funds are held by a trusted intermediary as per contract, until specific conditions are met. While it often involves custody, in some cases, smart contracts enforce the agreement, ensuring that assets or funds are released only when predetermined criteria are fulfilled, without relying on human intervention.

**ESG:** Environmental, Social, and Governance is an investment ideology that has departed from fundamentals and, thus, has largely resulted in poor performance. Proponents, like BlackRock, have shifted their ESG stance on Bitcoin due to growing interest. They criticised it initially for being "non-ESG compliant", while secretly building their massive position in it.

**EVM:** The Ethereum Virtual Machine serves as the computational engine at the core of the Ethereum blockchain. Being Turing-complete, the EVM processes and executes smart contracts, which are self-executing agreements written in Ethereum programming languages, like Solidity. Security comes from the consensus that runs via this bytecode execution.

**IOU:** An IOU (I Owe You) is a written or verbal acknowledgment of a debt or obligation, where one party promises to repay or provide something to another. IOUs are typically informal and may lack legal enforceability, making them non-binding agreements, often used among friends or family. Most of them will not have any legal standing in case of a dispute.

**Jailbreak:** The process of removing any software restrictions on a device, allowing users to make it do things that are not officially supported by the manufacturer. Geeks find it fun because it grants them more control and customisation, enabling the installation of "forbidden" programmes and the exploration of the device's full potential. However, it may void warranties.

**KYC-AML:** Know Your Customer and Anti-Money Laundering are financial regulations requiring institutions to verify and monitor customer identities and report suspicious activities. Critics argue that, while they aim to combat illegal financial activities, they can lead to privacy breaches exploited by scammers and the financial exclusion of marginalised groups.

**Legal Tender:** This refers to a form of money that national courts are required to recognise as satisfactory payment for any monetary debt. This settlement cannot be rejected by merchants. In some countries, non-traditional currencies have gained legal tender status, as in the case of El Salvador, which made BTC its second legal tender in 2021, alongside USD.

**L2:** Short for Layer 2, this refers to a secondary chain or scaling solution that operates on top of a primary chain, like Ethereum. L2 solutions aim to enhance scalability, reduce congestion, and, above all, lower transaction costs. They do so by bundling several transactions together on the secondary chain into a rollup, settled as one transaction on the primary.

**Mercantilism:** An economic theory of the 16th-18th centuries, which linked a nation's prosperity to amassing gold reserves. It advocated trade surpluses, export promotion, and tariffs to hoard gold, as this implied wealth and power. Gold focus influenced policy, driving nations to seek favourable trade balances and accumulate it as a shiny symbol of strength.

**Metaverse:** A virtual, interconnected, and immersive meta-universe, where users can interact, socialise, and engage in various activities. Imagine attending a metaverse concert, where you use an avatar to join others in a virtual venue, watching a live performance, chatting with friends, and even purchasing virtual merchandise. Just none of it is "real".

**NFT:** A Non-Fungible Token is a digital asset representing ownership or proof of authenticity of a unique item, often on a blockchain. Unlike cryptocurrencies, NFTs are indivisible and non-interchangeable, making them ideal for digital art, collectibles, music, and other digital creations, as they certify their scarcity and provenance. So, NFTs can certify documents.

**Node:** This is a computer or device that participates in the blockchain by validating or relaying transactions and blocks. Self-hosted node servers allow users to directly access and verify blockchain data. This increases their self-reliance and ensures the integrity of the whole network, by promoting more decentralisation and trust in that blockchain ecosystem.

**Plausible Deniability:** This refers to the ability to deny knowledge or involvement in an action, often by creating ambiguity or uncertainty. It is crucial in the context of financial freedom in challenging environments, as it allows individuals to conceal the full extent of their available resources, whether monetary or not, and protect themselves from persecution and prosecution.

**Proxychains:** These are used for routing internet connections through a series of proxy servers and are preferred by hackers over VPNs or TOR because they offer greater control over proxy selection. This allows them to mix different types, switch between them rapidly, and evade detection more effectively, enhancing their ability to carry out activities while staying hidden.

**P2P:** Peer-to-Peer refers to a decentralised network model where the participants or peers interact directly with each other without any intermediaries. This is commonly used in file sharing, cryptocurrency transactions, and private communication, enabling efficient and direct exchanges of information, assets, or services among the users involved.

**Smart Contracts:** Smart contracts are self-executing agreements with predefined rules and conditions, encoded on blockchain technology. Coined by Nick Szabo, they automate and enforce contract terms, eliminating intermediaries and providing transparency, security, and trust in applications including finance, supply chain, and many legal processes.

**Stealth Address:** Proposed by Vitalik Buterin, these are a privacy-enhancing feature coming to Ethereum. They will generate unique, one-time addresses for each transaction, obscuring the sender's identity and transaction details on the blockchain. This enhances privacy and security, as it makes it much harder to trace transactions back to any known users.

**UBO:** Ultimate Beneficial Owner refers to the individual(s) who ultimately own or control an entity, such as a company or trust, and benefit from its activities. Definitions of UBO and the specific criteria and regulations can differ significantly from one jurisdiction to another, but they generally aim to identify the real individuals behind any legal entity to "prevent abuse".

**Wallet:** Wallets are digital tools used in blockchain and cryptocurrency systems to "store", manage, and interact with digital assets. They securely save the private keys needed to access and control cryptocurrencies, enabling users to send, receive, and monitor their holdings on the blockchain. Coins are not stored in wallets, but on the blockchain ledger.

**Web3 DApp:** A Web3 Decentralised Application is a software application built on blockchain or decentralised technology, enabling Peer-to-Peer interactions without the need for intermediaries. It utilises smart contracts and other decentralised infrastructure, offering transparency, security, and more user control. These include DeFi platforms and NFT marketplaces.

# ABOUT THE AUTHORS

## Lev Mikulitski

**A strategist in the game called Life; Lev Mikulitski is a serial tech entrepreneur, a personal and business growth author, and a dedicated father of three children.**

Lev Mikulitski is a seasoned Strategic Planner, Growth Expert, and serial impact entrepreneur dedicated to shaping a vibrant and innovative future. With extensive hands-on experience in building and transforming businesses, Lev brings a dynamic force of passionate expertise to the table. His inquisitive mind constantly seeks to question and explore, embracing each experience as a stepping-stone towards ever-evolving success.

Drawing from a wealth of knowledge, Lev's managerial insights serve as a treasure trove, empowering individuals and businesses to take proactive steps today for future relevance and prosperity. As a happily married individual and proud parent of three children.

Lev's unwavering commitment to human evolution and community fuels his passion for innovation, strategy, and personal growth. This approach has consistently proven successful in helping businesses unlock their potential. With a mastery of embracing the unknown, Lev tackles business and personal challenges with a broader perspective, going beyond conventional boundaries. He has identified the essential pillars of success that must be established in both our professional and personal lives to create a truly meaningful impact on the world.

Lev holds a B.Sc. degree in Management from the Hebrew University in Jerusalem, an M.B.A. in Marketing (Magna Cum Laude), and various international diplomas from institutions such as Harvard Business School and London Business School. Furthermore, Lev has served as a lecturer on Consumer Behavior at the Hebrew University of Jerusalem in Israel and prestigious E-M.B.A. classes at Ben Gurion University in Israel, where he imparts his expertise in marketing.

Driven by truth, knowledge, professionalism, and an unwavering belief in the power of connection, Lev is rapidly establishing himself as a Strategic Business Expert of the future. With his sights set on "what's next" and a wealth of insights derived from transforming small businesses, he possesses the profound ability to turn dreams into reality on both personal and professional levels for his clients and followers. Lev's journey is a process of continuous discovery, brimming with exciting solutions.

Today, Lev invests his time in his family and his three children. As an inspiration, he is currently developing an educational-developmental brand for children called Mr. Who. This special project aims to foster the development of soft skills, critical thinking, and creativity through short stories featuring John, the hero of the book. More information about this project can be found on the website www.mrwho.me.

Lev is also involved in managing Mikulitski Creative Ventures Ltd, an American company that owns the brand "Mr. Who". Furthermore, he holds a partnership in Mellifex, a UK-based LLP, and serves as a partner and CBO in YieldX, an Israeli deep-tech startup in the field of animal health.

Lev's other books on personal and business growth include titles such as "MIND BLAST", "Deceptive Warfare", "Better Than Money", "Dad Bod Revolution", and two books under the "Mr. Who" brand.


## Matías (Matityahu) Monteagudo

**A Spanish serial entrepreneur, crypto philanthropist, and privacy activist who co-founded Mellifex LLP, the first non-custodial escrow technology for crypto transactions.**

Matías (Matityahu) Monteagudo is a Spanish serial entrepreneur, privacy activist, crypto philanthropist, and non-fiction author, born in 1992. His father is a psychologist and inventor with patents to his name, while his mother is a philologist, who contributed to the creation of one of Spain's most widely used dictionaries, having devoted her life's work to teaching.

Once an autistic child, Matías possesses an unquenchable curiosity, he just wants to know. This would lead to a life of experimentation, one in which he always sought to become a polymath of the Renaissance. His earliest known interests, as a teenager, were in the fields of architecture and then, later on, music... His personal favorite being John Zorn's avant-garde!

In his last college years, he got hooked on behavioral economics, namely the auction theory of Paul Milgrom and Robert Wilson, who would both be eventually awarded the Nobel Memorial Prize in Economic Sciences. Not long after graduating, Matías found blockchain and was captivated by the possibilities of this technology, bootstrapping his first crypto businesses.

He co-founded Mellifex LLP, together with the more veteran founders Lev Mikulitski and Fred Meyer. At the time, their payments innovation became the world's first purely non-custodial escrow, ensuring cryptoassets were securely locked on the public ledger of a blockchain as per contract, with safety mechanisms to control the outcome, e.g. timelock, arbitration, etc.

Having navigated the "seven seas" of crypto for a decade and surviving, Matías is intimately involved with several protocols in different degrees of development. He never shies away from a worthy challenge to test new hypotheses in practice. Banking Unchained: How Cryptocurrencies Can Transform Your Financial Life was co-authored in an educational effort.

His Stichting Monteagudo Foundation stewards the Monteagudo family office, patronises Hebrew cultural heritage, endows the Jewish community with free loans, helps law enforcement root out anti-Semitism, grows Biblical forests to combat desertification, researches and advocates in matters of Haskalah, and brings endangered Israelites back to safety.

Lately, Matías has been helping some lawmakers and provided technical advice to institutions such as the European Supervisory Authorities (EBA, EIOPA, and ESMA) among others, on behalf of the industry. One of these consultations was Digital Operational Resilience Act (DORA), contributed in collaboration with the Blockchain Arbitration & Commerce Society (BACS).

www.ingramcontent.com/pod-product-compliance
Lightning Source LLC
Chambersburg PA
CBHW080111010626
45794CB00016B/3642